MUDBRICK SETTLEMENTS OF THE OMAN PENINSULA

sidestonepress

MUDBRICK SETTLEMENTS OF THE OMAN PENINSULA

Inhabited – Abandoned – Re(dis)covered

Stephanie Döpper, Birgit Mershen, Josephine Kanditt,
Irini Biezeveld & Thomas Schmidt-Lux (eds)

Published by Sidestone Press, Leiden
www.sidestone.com
E-mail: info @ sidestone.nl
Phone: (+31)(0)71-7370131

Lay-out & cover design: Sidestone Press
Photograph cover: Birkat al Mawz, Al Dakhiliyah, Oman (front photo: Christophe Cappelli, stock.adobe.com); back photo: Irini Biezeveld).

ISBN 978-94-6426-401-2 (softcover)
ISBN 978-94-6426-402-9 (hardcover)
ISBN 978-94-6426-403-6 (PDF e-book)

DOI: 10.59641/j0m6g7h8i9

Gedruckt mit Unterstützung der Gerda Henkel Stiftung, Düsseldorf

GERDA HENKEL STIFTUNG

Contents

Introduction

Mudbrick Settlements of the Oman Peninsula: Inhabited – Abandoned – Re(dis)covered

Stephanie Döpper, Birgit Mershen, Josephine Kanditt, Irini Biezeveld and Thomas Schmidt-Lux

Oman's landscape is dotted with abandoned mudbrick settlements and quarters, known as *ḥārāt*, either isolated in the countryside or surrounded by vibrant, modern urban centres. While some were abandoned more than a century ago, the greatest wave of abandonment came with the economic upturn and opening of the country after Sultan Qaboos bin Said came to power in 1970. As the country modernised, many of the old mudbrick houses were abandoned and new modern concrete houses were built instead. This move from traditional to modern houses led to the deterioration and decay of the physical substance of the mudbrick buildings. In the face of these conditions, various Omani and international actors have repeatedly warned against the uncontrolled loss of this valuable cultural heritage. The former inhabitants of the mudbrick houses and their descendants have also repeatedly emphasised their emotional attachment to these abandoned places and their personal significance to them. This has led to several recording projects and ethnological studies by the Ministry of Heritage and Tourism of the Sultanate of Oman and international research teams to document the past before it disappears (e.g., Ministry of Heritage and Culture 2013; 2014a; 2014b; 2014c; Ministry of Tourism 2016; Al Abri 2014; Al Jahwari 2006; Bandyopadhyay 2005a; 2005b; Bandyopadhyay – Sibley 2003; Bandyopadhyay *et al.* 2013; Benkari 2017; Bonnenfant *et al.* 1977; Damluji 1998; Gaube – Gangler 2012; Ibrahim – ElMahi 1998; Klinger 2021; Korn 2008a; 2008b; Le Cour Grandmaison 1977; Mershen 1999; 2001; 2002; Nagieb *et al.* 2004; Ribbeck *et al.* 2001; Sachedina 2013; Scholz 1984; 2014). At the same time, others, especially tourists, have glorified the dilapidated state of the ruins as an aesthetically beautiful backdrop for a romanticised vision of the past, and more recently, some of these mudbrick settlements are experiencing a revival as tourist destinations, fuelled by the economic challenges and travel restrictions during the Covid-19 pandemic (e.g., Mershen *et al.* 2025). Tourist perception, revitalisation and also archaeological research that goes beyond an architectural focus have rarely been the focus of academic research (but see Whitcomb 1975; Young *et al.* 2018; Young 2019). The mudbrick settlements of Oman are thus ostensibly abandoned, but at the same time they are an important object of conflicting processes of interpretation and negotiation. They are caught between the poles of remembering and forgetting, glorification and neglect.

This was the starting point for the interdisciplinary research project "The abandoned mudbrick settlements of central Oman: Between romanticisation and neglect", funded by the Gerda Henkel Foundation as part of the "Lost Cities" programme between 2020 and 2022, which was conducted by sociologists Thomas Schmidt-Lux and Josephine Kanditt (University of Leipzig), Islamic studies scholar Birgit Mershen (Ruhr University Bochum) and archaeologists Stephanie Döpper and Irini Biezeveld (then Goethe University Frankfurt). This book is the proceedings of the final conference of the project, in which team members present the results of the project and leading experts give papers on inhabited, abandoned and re(dis)covered mudbrick settlements in the Sultanate of Oman.

The chapters of the book adopt a diachronic perspective, examining the past, present and future of the *ḥārāt*. This structure aligns with disciplinary views on the topic, which range from archaeology, ethnography and sociology. In the first chapter, Stephanie Döpper and Irini Biezeveld discuss the life histories of 21 mudbrick settlements in a selected area in the Wilayat Al Mudhaybi. The settlements can be divided according to their size, layout and economic functions as services they provided. This includes regional centres with multiple *ḥārāt* and/or a souq, compact sites with one settlement area, a regular layout and a clear defensive structure, small hamlets with scattered buildings and non-domestic sites such as forts. Based on fieldwork, including site visits, archaeological surface artefact collections, and small-scale archaeological excavations at selected sites, it can be demonstrated that different waves of abandonment are evident within these mudbrick settlements. The two main ones are at the turn of the 19th to 20th century and post-1970. Consequently, the abandonment of the historic mudbrick settlements cannot be attributed to a single cause, namely the modernisation during the reign of Sultan Qaboos (*nahḍa*). Rather, it can be demonstrated that there were a number of social, economic and political factors at play throughout time.

In the second chapter, Ruth Young examines the role of abandoned, derelict structures in the formation of individual and social memory, as well as in fostering a sense of belonging among those who previously inhabited them. She draws upon the research conducted between 2012 and 2016 as part of the "Bat Oasis Historical Archaeology Project" at the mudbrick village of Bat. Her research was conducted through archaeological planning, excavations, building analyses, and interviews with former inhabitants. In synthesising the disparate forms of evidence and methodologies, Young traces the transition from mudbrick houses as physical structures to the repositories of memory of a way of life that has now undergone a permanent transformation.

Ali Al Mahrouqi presents in the third chapter the efforts by the Ministry of Heritage and Tourism in documenting recording and protecting the historic buildings of the Sultanate of Oman through the creation of a database with an on-site inventory of 1,050 sites and thorough expert documentation of selected *ḥārāt* such as Harat Al Saybani in Birkat Al Mawz and Harat Al Yaman in Izki. This allowed the classification into three different categories according to structural conditions of the site resulting in a development agenda. Nevertheless, challenges to the preservation of the traditional architecture in the Sultanate of Oman still prevail, both natural and man-made, such as weathering, the absence of regular maintenance, biodeterioration and the rapid urbanisation of the country.

In the fourth chapter, Birgit Mershen discusses the changes in the meaning and perception of the abandoned mudbrick residential quarters, since the Omani *nahḍa* in the 1970s and asks whether currently expanding private and municipal initiatives may be understood as a kind of reconquest, in the sense that former residents and their descendants are making the *ḥāra* their own again, feeling a renewed emotional connection to it as well as comprehending the *ḥāra* as identity-establishing. Or should current processes be understood as a rediscovery or as a reinvention of the *ḥāra*. These questions are addressed by discussing the chief elements defining the *ḥārāt* as residential quarters and outlining of the sociocultural effects associated with the move out of traditional neighbourhoods to newly developed residential areas in the last quarter of the 20th century. Examining the diverse official, scholarly and civil *ḥārāt* discourse and practices during the first two decades of the 21st century and in the age of the renewed "Renaissance" proclaimed by Sultan Haitham bin Tariq upon his succession to the throne in January 2020, the chapter explores the dynamics of a shifting discourse, practices and the different actors associated with current trends in the *ḥārāt* restoration and adaptive reuse.

Soumyen Bandyopadhyay's and Claudia Briguglio's chapter looks at the physical characteristics of Harat al-ʿAqr, the historic core of the ancient oasis of Nizwa, and how they have been shaped by physical, socio-political and cultural forces over time. Special emphasis is placed on the urban artefacts and artistic traditions: the decorated *miḥrāb*, the construction of the city wall and timber crafting. It explores how all this is linked to tradition and the historical imamates in Nizwa and Oman's maritime traditions. In doing so, the chapter demonstrates the importance of the regulatory framework for preserving the urban and architectural heritage of Harat al-ʿAqr in the ongoing conservation and transformation approached in relation to heritage tourism.

In the sixth chapter, Thomas Schmidt-Lux and Josephine Kanditt look at the visibility of the *ḥārāt* from a primarily touristic perspective. The authors combine their observations from field research with theoretical considerations on visibility and invisibility. Systematically, they want to ask how the Omani settlements actually become visible and what meanings they acquire in the process. This also includes the question of what is not shown. By no means is the same visibility granted to all *ḥārāt*, rather, there is a clear hierarchy in the visibility of settlements; in other words, some settlements are clearly privileged by the tourist gaze. However, one of the authors' key findings shows that there is no one dominant interpretation in the tourist perception of the *ḥārāt*. Rather, the different examples show how varied the *ḥārāt* appear and are interpreted.

In the final chapter, Heike Delitz discusses how architecture influences social structures focussing on the spectacle. Looking at the traditional architecture in Oman, she comes to the conclusion that both the spectacle of the decaying *ḥārāt* on the one hand, and the spectacle of a cultural heritage on the other, are tools to imaginarily institute a national identity which not only overwrites tribal affiliations, but also presents them as preceding it. Delitz labels this politics as "architecture against the tribes".

Two additional papers by Michaela Hoffmann-Ruf on "Al-Sūr al-Muḥīṭ: The City Wall of Bahla as a Case Study for the Organization of Communal Tasks in Central Oman on the Eve of Modern State Administration, 1967–1976" and by Hamda Al Hajri on "Beauty of the Past: Analysis Towards an Oasis Settlement in Oman as a Prototype for Future Development" were presented during the conference as well. For different reasons, such as publication elsewhere (Buessow – Hoffmann-Ruf – Al Saqri 2023), they are not included in these proceedings.

References

Al Abri, H. N. S. 2014
Urban pattern and architecture of traditional Omani foothill settlements: Al-Hamrā and Birkat al-Mawz [PhD thesis, Nottingham Trent University].

Al Jahwari, N. 2006
Ancient quarters in Oman: An urgency in the archaeology of Oman, in: Ministry of Heritage and Culture – UNESCO World Heritage Centre (eds), *Proceedings of the Regional Seminar on the Conservation of Earthen Structures in the Arab Countries*, Muscat, 35–44.

Bandyopadhyay, S. 2005a
Diversity in unity: An analysis of the settlement structure of Ḥārat al-ʿAqr, Nizwā (Oman), *Proceedings of the Seminar for Arabian Studies* 35, 19–36.

Bandyopadhyay, S. 2005b
Problematic aspects of synthesis and interpretation in the study of traditional Omani built environment, in: T. Shakur (ed.), *Cities in transition: transforming the global built environment*, Open House Press, 16–28.

Bandyopadhyay, S. – Quattrone, G. – Al Abri, H. N. 2013
In times of war: Typological and morphological characteristics of dwellings in Ḥārat al-Yemen in Izkī, Oman, *Proceedings of the Seminar for Arabian Studies* 43, 27–45.

Bandyopadhyay, S. – Sibley, M. 2003
The distinctive typology of central Omani mosques: its nature and antecedents, *Proceedings of the Seminar for Arabian Studies* 33, 99–116.

Benkari, N. 2017
The defensive vernacular settlements in Oman, a contextual study, *International Journal of Heritage Architecture* 1/2, 175–184. DOI:10.2495/ha-v1-n2-175-184

Bonnenfant, P. – Bonnenfant, G. – Al-Harthi, S. 1977
Architecture and social history at Mudayrib, *The Journal of Oman Studies* 3/2, 107–135.

Büssow, J. – Hoffmann-Ruf, M. – Al Saqri, N. 2023
Al-Sūr al-Muḥīṭ. The city wall of Bahla as a case study for the organisation of communal tasks in central Oman on the eve of modern state administration, 1967–1977, Bonner Islamstudien 47, Berlin.

Damluji, S. S. 1998
The architecture of Oman, Reading.

Gaube, H. – Gangler, A. 2012
Transformation processes in oasis settlements of Oman, Muscat.

Ibrahim, M. – ElMahi, A. 1998
Two seasons of SQU investigation at Wadi as-Safafir (1996-1997), *Proceedings of the Seminar for Arabian Studies* 25, 125–137.

Klinger, T. 2021
L'Oman contemporain: Aménagement du territoire et identité nationale, Berlin.

Korn, L. 2008a
Fortifications and palaces, in: A. Al Salimi – H. Gaube – L. Korn (eds.), *Islamic art in Oman*, Muscat, 118–151.

Korn, L. 2008b
Religious architecture, in: A. Al Salimi – H. Gaube – L. Korn (eds.), *Islamic art in Oman*, Muscat, 60–105.

Le Cour Grandmaison, C. 1977
Spatial organisation, tribal groupings and kinship in Ibra, *The Journal of Oman Studies* 3/2, 95–106.

Mershen, B. 1999
Settlement space and architecture in South-Arabian oases: Preliminary remarks on the use and division of space in Omani oasis settlements, *Proceedings of the Seminar for Arabian Studies* 29, 103–110.

Mershen, B. 2001
Observations on the archaeology and ethnohistory of rural estates of the 17th through early 20th centuries in Oman. *Proceedings of the Seminar for Arabian Studies* 31, 145–160.

Mershen, B. 2002
"Let the water run back". Archaeological and ethnohistorical observations from Wadi Fanjah/Wadi al-Khod, Oman: The case of a failed 18th/19th century agro-economic enterprise, *Proceedings of the Seminar for Arabian Studies* 32, 99–116.

Mershen, B. – Kanditt, J. – Schmidt-Lux, T. – Döpper, S. – Biezeveld, I. 2025
Harat al Hamra: The journey from an oasis town to a 'heritage village', *Journal of Arabian Studies*. DOI: 10.1080/21534764.2024.2448042

Ministry of Heritage and Culture 2013
Harat Al-Aqr (Bahla): Documentation and Heritage Management Plan, Muscat.

Ministry of Heritage and Culture 2014a
Documentation and heritage management and development plan for Birkat Al-Mawz: Harat as-Saybani, Muscat.

Ministry of Heritage and Culture 2014b
Documentation and heritage management plan for Izki: Harat al-Yemen, Muscat.

Ministry of Heritage and Culture 2014c
Sinaw: Harat al-Burashdi & Harat al-Suwawfah. Documentation and heritage management plan, Muscat.

Ministry of Tourism 2016
Al-Hamra: Misfat al-Abriyin. Tourism development plan, Muscat.

Nagieb, M. – Siebert, S. – Luedeling, E. – Buerkert, A. – Häser, J. 2004
Settlement history of a mountain oasis in Northern Oman: Evidence from land-use and archaeological studies, *Die Erde* 135/1, 81–106.

Ribbeck, E. – Gangler, A. – Langend, U. (eds.) 2001
Oasis settlement in Oman. Pilot study 1999-2000, Stuttgart.

Sachedina, A. 2013
Of living traces and revived legacies: Unfolding futures in the Sultanate of Oman [PhD thesis, University of California, Berkley].

Scholz, F. 1984
Falaj-Oasen in Sharqiya, Inner-Oman, *Die Erde* 115, 273–294.

Scholz, F. 2014
Muscat then and now: Geographical sketch of a unique Arab town, Muscat/Berlin.

Young, R. 2019
Historical archaeology and heritage in the Middle East, London.

Young, R. – Al-Jassassi, A. – Al-Shaqsi, A. – Al-Jabri, S. – Batchelor, O. – Dance, K. – De Leon, N. – Humes, A. – Hunt, H. – Riaz, A. – Taha, S. – Cable, C. – Thornton, C. – Zäuner, S. 2018
Bat Oasis Historical Archaeology Project: Interim report on 2014 field season, *The Journal of Oman Studies* 19, 1–18.

Life Histories of Mudbrick Settlements in Central Oman

Stephanie Döpper and Irini Biezeveld

Introduction

Late Islamic (1650–1970 CE) mudbrick settlements are a ubiquitous feature in the central Omani landscape. Most archaeological and historical research has concentrated on individual sites, especially important regional, political, and economic centres (for a recent summary of these works, see Biezeveld 2022). This chapter presents the archaeological part of the Lost Cities Project. This project, funded by the Gerda Henkel Foundation, aimed to analyse the current condition, contrast between contemporary and previous use, and analyse the public perception of mudbrick settlements in Oman. This was done through an interdisciplinary approach, including sociology and Islamic studies. The archaeological part of the project focused on the micro-region around the modern city Al Mudhaybi in the Al Sharqiyah North governorate and paid special attention to smaller sites.

In this chapter, the life history of the mudbrick settlements in the micro-region of Al Mudhaybi will be investigated from their foundation, use, and abandonment as well as reuse and incorporation into the modern settlement pattern. A life history approach in archaeology started with the concepts of the social lives or biographies of objects (Appadurai 1986; Kopytoff 1986). Following Kopytoff (1986), objects have "social lives" and form histories through their life cycle. Schiffer (1972), who investigated the concept in order to understand the contexts of the deposition of the objects, also investigated the concept of life histories (studies that focussed on the social relationships between people and things followed Gosdon – Marshall 1999; Holtorf 2002; Overholtzer – Stoner 2011). The life history approach with regard to buildings is done to understand the deposition of house-related depositions (Reniere – De Clerq 2018). A house can be seen as more than its architecture, it is an artefact with some particular social aspects (Samson 1990). Also adapting the concept of Kopytoff (1986), Gerritsen (1999) applied the concept of cultural biography to fit houses and farmsteads and to consider the complete life cycle of archaeological sites. Understanding the cultural biography or life history of settlements is key to understanding the practices that created the archaeological record and the relationships between a house and its inhabitants. We are trying to apply this approach to the micro-region Al Mudhaybi to present a case study of the construction, habitation, abandonment and reuse cycles.

in: S. Döpper – B. Mershen – J. Kanditt – I. Biezeveld – T. Schmidt-Lux (eds) 2025, *Mudbrick Settlements of the Oman Peninsula. Inhabited – Abandoned – Re(dis)covered*, Leiden: Sidestone Press, 13–32.

Methodology

The study area for the micro-regional analysis of the changes in settlement use from the Late Islamic period (1650–1970 CE) until modern day concentrates on a roughly 30 × 30 km area in the surroundings of the modern town of Al Mudhaybi, capital of the Wilaya by the same name in the Al Sharqiyah North governorate of the Sultanate of Oman. This region is characterised by two large wadi systems, Wadi Andam and Wadi Samad, crossing the area from north to south, and a smaller third one, the Wadi Al Ithili. The latter cuts through the western part of the Al Hammah mountain. In addition to the Lost Cities Project, the region has been subject to a multi-period archaeological survey conducted between 2018 and 2022, which besides many prehistoric structures also documented features from the Late Islamic period (Döpper – Schmidt 2020; Döpper 2022a; Döpper 2022b; Döpper 2023).

During the Al Mudhaybi Regional Survey, Late Islamic mudbrick settlements were identified through remote sensing based on freely available satellite images and recorded as polygons in a geographical information system (QGIS). A total of 21 different mudbrick sites were identified this way, where in some cases (Sinaw, Al Mukhtara) they represent individual *ḥāra* of the same settlement. Additionally, the satellite imagery was used to map *falaj* systems. This information was combined with data on wadi courses provided by the National Survey Authority of the Sultanate of Oman. In 2022, all sites were briefly visited by the authors. Additionally, a detailed study of five selected sites was carried out in the framework of the Lost Cities Project between 2020 and 2022. These sites are Al Milayh, Al Mintarib, Al Qabrayn, Safrat Al Khashbah, and Al Washhi North (Biezeveld 2023). These sites were studied in more detail because they were completely abandoned, with no modern-day building activities in the surroundings, which would present the authors with an undisturbed image of a Late Islamic archaeological dataset. These sites also reflected various types of use in the past and with different signs of reuse.

The detailed study of these five settlements was done through an archaeological survey and small-scale excavation. The survey included a description of the architectural features at these sites and photographic documentation. Additionally, all the archaeological finds associated with the architectural features were collected and measured with a GPS device (Garmin eTrex 10). At four of the sites, test trenches of 1 × 2 m were excavated. The trenches were located so that they crossed two rooms. This was done to see whether there was a difference in the deposition and to see whether there were multiple construction phases. The main goal of these test trenches was to obtain radiocarbon dates and data on the use-life of the sites. It is always assumed that the Late Islamic sites date to the Yaʿariba investments in the 17th century and that they were abandoned in the 1970s, but this has never been confirmed by radiocarbon dates. Additionally, the radiocarbon dates also provide a more precise range for the dating of the finds that are associated with the layers.

After the documentation, survey, and excavation in the field, the finds were processed. The small finds were drawn and described in the project's database. The undiagnostic ceramics (undecorated body sherds) were assigned a ceramic ware in the database, and the diagnostic sherds were drawn and described in more detail in the database. The diagnostic sherds were assigned to a vessel type (i.e., bowls, cups, pots, flasks) and were assigned to a specific form type. The form type is based on the anatomic division of a ceramic vessel: the rim, the neck, the shoulder, body, lower body, base and foot, where the definition of the form typology goes from top to bottom (Döpper 2019). It classifies the characteristics of the shape of the vessel. The form type was then combined with the ceramic ware, resulting in the ware-form type, and a ceramic typology for the study area was made. Based on the ware-form type, parallels in previously published material were sought to create an understanding of where similar sherds were found, in which contexts and what possible age they have.

Additionally, historical and ethnographic sources concerning the Late Islamic period were consulted to get a general idea of the period and settlements in central Oman. These accounts were written by diplomats or political agents from the British Government (Hugh-Thomas 1856; Lorimer 1908; Miles 1896; Miles 1919), from a scholarly perspective (Landen 1967; Scholz 1977; Scholz 1984; Stiffe 1897; Wellsted 1838), and from a traveller's perspective (Morris 1957). Accounts from Arab historians were not available to the authors or were read as citations in other publications. With regard to the research area, there are few mentions in these accounts. These generally included the central Oman region, but case studies within the research area were mostly not mentioned. What is remarkable is that Wellsted (1838), who travelled through the interior of Oman passing through Samad and Nizwa, has no mention of Sinaw or Al Mudhaybi, which would have been the largest centres in the study area. Morrison, who travelled from Adam to the Jebel Al Akhdar in central Oman, also makes no mention of the rest of central Oman, and Miles (1910), who travelled from Samail to Manah to Adam and back, also seems to be unaware of what occurs in the research area.

Mudbrick settlements in the Al Mudhaybi region

In the research area, 21 mudbrick settlements are found along the courses of Wadi Andam, Wadi Samad and Wadi Al Ithili (Fig. 1). This distribution pattern is easily

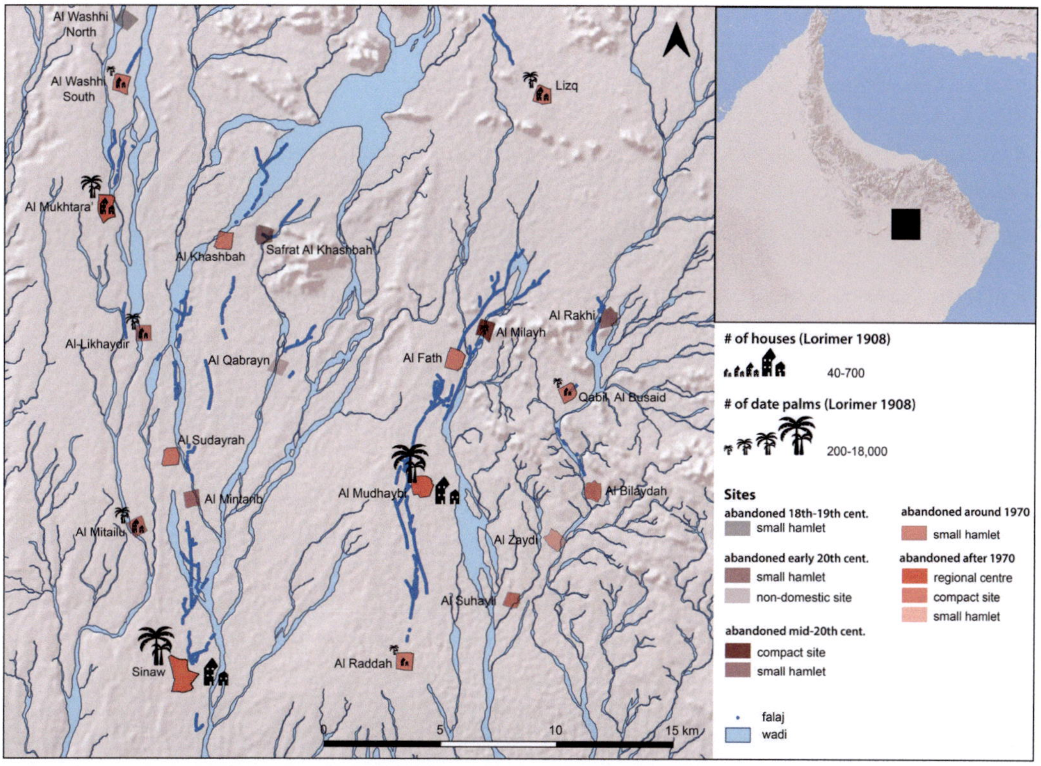

Fig. 1: Map of the research area with mudbrick settlements mentioned in the text, their type and date of abandonment.

explained by the availability of water, especially when considering that the agricultural land of those sites was irrigated though *daudi aflāj* systems, where the water source is one or more mother wells dug deep into a wadi bottom up to 17 km upstream from the settlement (Al Ghafri 2018). The settlements differ both in size and layout as well as in economic function and services provided. For this chapter, we have divided the settlements in four different groups based on size and function. These are: (1) regional centres that consist of multiple *ḥārāt* and/or have a souq, (2) compact sites that consist of one quarter and have a regular layout and a clear defensive structure, (3) small hamlets that consist of scattered buildings and (4) non-domestic sites with main functions other than domestic.

Regional centres

The largest regional centre in the research area is Sinaw with its six well defined *ḥārāt* east of the modern city of Sinaw and the souq. Sinaw (Sanāu) is described by Lorimer as a town of nearly 3,500 inhabitants that live in 660 houses of mud, which have multiple storeys. There were 18,000 date palms (Lorimer 1908: 1682). Scholz (1977) mentioned that in the oasis, Bedouins rented or owned areas, where they would live in summer. Architectural documentation of Sinaw was conducted in two *ḥārāt* by ArCHIAM and the Ministry of Heritage and Culture in 2014. They conducted a detailed study, documenting all the architectural features of the *ḥārāt* and developing heritage management plans for future purposes of the sites. Within the Harat Al Barashid, the buildings were mostly constructed of mudbrick on a stone foundation, or in some cases also the lower stories were built completely out of stone and rendered with mud or clay plaster (Ministry of Heritage and Culture 2014: 34). The dwellings ranged from one to three stories. Two structures looked like a mini-fortress complete with a gate tower and parapet walls. The *ḥāra* could only be accessed by one gate and there was a substantial wall formation as well as several towers. Harat Al Sawafah is the northernmost *ḥāra* in the Sinaw oasis. It could be entered through three gates on the northern and southern sides. The *ḥāra* was organized around a rectangular central square, from which the roads spread out in a somewhat orthogonal way. There seemed to be generally more space than in Harat Al Barashid. The whole *ḥāra* is characterized by arches, courtyards and high-quality *sarooj* and the dwellings were made of mudbrick and stones. Half of the dwellings had two floors, and very few had a third floor. In total, there were four mosques (Ministry of Heritage and Culture 2014: 57, 63). South of this *ḥāra* lies Harat Al Rashidi, and southwest of this lies the settlement cluster including Hillat Al Qalah, Hillat Al Suq and Al Arqub. These had not been documented in previous literature.

The second largest site is Al Mudhaybi. It is described by Lorimer (1908) as a town of 700 houses and the second largest place in the Sharqiyah after Ibra, with a population of 3,500 or more. People from four different tribes inhabited the town. There were about 10,000 date palms as well as livestock (Lorimer 1908: 1245). It is also mentioned by Scholz (1977) as an oasis where Bedouins owned or rented parts of the oases. They lived there during the summer. At the end of the date season, the Bedouin living in the oases would move to the Indian Ocean coastal areas, whereas the settled people living in the mudbrick villages would live there all year round. At the coast, fish was caught which was partly sold at the weekly markets of Sinaw and Al Mudbaybi (Scholz 1977: 126). Architecturally, it was described by Damluji (1998) who visited the town in 1995 and 1997. The settlement was surrounded by a wall, which can be entered through two gates. Inside the old town, there are Harat Al Jawabir and Hillat Al Suq. The old market, Souq Al Masila, is still in operation. Damluji focussed her description on Bait Al ʻUd, an imposing fort-like mansion in Harat Al Jawabir. The house was built in Harat Al Jawabir in the 1960s, and she met the builders and original owners of the house who gave her a detailed description of how the house was built (Damluji 1998: 343–344). Today, modern construction can be seen within the old settlement, but the majority of the traditional houses remain as ruins and are sometimes visited or used by previous owners or family members.

A site with two distinct mudbrick quarters is Al Mukhtara (Fig. 2). Both are situated west of the cultivated oasis and north of the modern village. The southern one, Al Hijrah, is larger, following a regular rectangular layout with modern buildings overbuilding the traditional architecture in its corners. Some of the mudbrick houses are currently used as animal pens. Attempts for renovations with concrete and electrification in the now abandoned and partially collapsed houses (Fig. 2b) speak in favour of an abandonment of the site post-1970. Although no longer visible, the layout suggests the settlement was once walled. In its north-east, there is the completely refurbished Al Hijrah mosque. South of it are the ruins of a trapezoidal-shaped building referred to as the old souq. The northern quarter, Al Daffa, is small, but originally also seems to have been encompassed by a wall. In this area, copper slag is scattered on the surface. Surface pottery in both *ḥārāt* include Bahla Ware (Živković *et al.* 2019), Comb-Incised White Ware (Power 2015) and modern (semi-)porcelains (Grey 2011) (Fig. 2e). The quarter is mentioned in Lorimer's gazetteer as having 100 houses and 2,000 date palms (Lorimer 1908: 78).

Fig. 2: Al Mukhtara. Brown = mudbrick houses, white = concrete houses.

Compact sites

Generally smaller in overall size, but similarly having a regular layout, are the villages of Al Raddah, Qabil Al Busaid, Al Khashbah, Al Milayh, Al Washhi South, Lizq and Al Sudayrah. Al Raddah follows the typical, regular layout of what Scholz (1984) refers to as a street settlement (*Straßensiedlung*). The *falaj* comes in from the north, goes through the settlement via the straight central street and opens into the oasis. Some of the old buildings are still in use today, reinforced by concrete and mainly rented out to South Asian workers. In the south-western corner, there is a well-maintained mudbrick tower overlooking the oasis and the settlement. Although not much of the wall that once surrounded the settlement remains, some gates are still preserved (Fig. 3a, e). They feature a typical vaulted space (*sabla*) furnished with built-in benches (Benkari 2017; Damluji 1998; Ministry of Heritage and Culture 2014). In the north, there is the house of the Sheikh's family (Fig. 3c–d). Sheikhly houses usually had a fortified appearance to reflect the important social position of the Sheikh and were used to protect the village's inhabitants during times of conflict (Benkari 2017: 181; Damluji 1998: 258; Young 2019; Wellsted 1838: 79–80). It was inhabited until a few years ago by family members and today mainly used as a sheep and goat pen. Next to it, there is the completely renovated and still used Sharia Mosque. Another mosque, the Saif bin Nasser bin Amer Al Jabri Mosque, is located further south inside the settlement. This has also been renovated, but more of its traditional layout remains, including a single dome (*būmah*) on the north-east corner, which acts as a small built-in minaret (Damluji 1998: 295). The mosque also has a prayer niche (*miḥrāb*) that occurs often and only in the interior of Oman (Benkari 2022). This type of *miḥrāb* consists of receding arches within the payer niche (Damluji 1998: 226). Al Raddah was described by Lorimer (1908: 1767) as having 40 houses and 600 date palms.

Fig. 3: Al Raddah. Brown = mudbrick houses, white = concrete houses.

Qabil Al Busaid is a compact, more or less rectangular, well-organised mudbrick quarter, surrounded by a wall and equipped with a free-standing tower. Lorimer (1908: 1767) mentioned it under Qabil Bani Bu Sa'id. The settlement consisted of 40 houses and was described as being deserted in 1905 on account of drought. There were 200 palm trees. It is also mentioned by Scholz (1977) as an oasis where Bedouins owned or rented parts of the oasis. Today it sits in between the modern buildings of the village and its oasis. The tower is the tallest standing building and was kept up or renovated after the abandonment of the mudbrick houses. It has its entrance on the first floor, which is common in central Oman (Bonnenfant *et al.* 1997: 118; Ministry of Tourism 2016: 35). To underline its defensive function, the tower was equipped with holes for shooting (*mrāq*) and battlements on top of the watchtower (Bonnenfant *et al.* 1997; Damluji 1998; Gaube – Gangler 2012). Although less clear than Al Raddah, it also fits the category of a street settlement. Inhabitants of the modern Qabil Al Busaid still remember their grandparents living in the mudbrick houses.

Al Milayh is a rectangular mudbrick settlement which is surrounded by a wall and which has a free-standing tower in the middle of the settlement. The oasis is located to the west of the village and is separated from it by a wadi-bed. There are no modern buildings in its vicinity, except a handful of farms. The tower is very similar to the tower at Qabil Al Busaid, also having its entrance on the first floor as well as the other architectural elements. Also, at Al Milayh, the tower was kept up or renovated after the abandonment of the settlement. In the oasis, there is a renovated mosque in the traditional central Omani style with a *būmah* (Biezeveld 2023). It was described by Lorimer (1908: 1767) as "Milaih". He noted that the town was deserted and that there were 600 date trees in the oasis.

Al Washhi South is surrounded by a cultivated oasis and some modern-day houses. There is a *falaj* coming from the north, which passes the still-used mosque before entering the abandoned mudbrick village. Next to modern-day buildings, concrete refurbishments could be seen at some of the mudbrick structures, indicating that it was likely abandoned during or after the 1970s. The houses are still preserved up to two storeys and the tower is also in good shape, which would also speak for a recent abandonment of the settlement. Lorimer mentions it in his gazetteer, noting that the site had 50 houses and 600 date palms (Lorimer 1908: 78).

Despite the considerable size of the modern town of Lizq, its mudbrick core is rather small, surrounding a rocky outcrop that is topped by a tower. The tower is renovated and illuminated at night. Directly surrounding the tower, the traditional houses can still be seen, but hardly 50 metres away from the tower, modern construction starts. This includes a mosque, a supermarket and houses. The mudbrick houses also showed much evidence of refurbishment with concrete. Although not much remains due to modern overbuilding, the settlement is likely to have been walled in the past. In layout, it also seems to have been a street settlement.

Al Sudayrah differs from the other sites discussed before as it is surrounded on all sites by the currently cultivated oasis. Most of its surrounding wall is still preserved. No modern houses are within the old settlement area; they are only found on the outskirts of the oasis. The mosque at its northern end is the building that was maintained the longest and is thus the best preserved. It features a typical *miḥrāb* with multiple receding arches (Fig. 4d) as well as the *būmah* (Bandyopadhyay – Sibley 2004; Damluji 1998) (Fig. 4e). Right in front of the mosque, a small ablution structure above the *falaj* is preserved. One of the entrances to the settlement on its western side is guarded by a well preserved square fortified gate

Fig. 4: Al Sudayrah. Brown = mudbrick houses.

(Fig. 4b). The gate is equipped with holes for shooting (*mrāq*) and battlements, underlining its defensive function (Bonnenfant *et al.* 1997; Damluji 1998; Gaube – Gangler 2012). Square watchtowers are less common than the round watchtowers. However, square towers for gates are often found in central Oman (Bandyopadhyay 2004; Damluji 1998; Ministry of Heritage and Culture 2014). The overall good preservation with many buildings still standing two storeys tall indicates that the houses were given up post-1970s (Fig. 4c). However, little modernization efforts in terms of concrete or electrification is visible.

Little can be said about Al Fath as its mudbrick core is nearly completely overbuilt by modern houses. Therefore, the original layout and extent are uncertain. As one gate remained, it is clear that the settlement once was walled. It is situated north of the presently cultivated oasis and was likely of the street settlement type. The mudbrick settlement of Al Khashbah is similarly partially overbuilt by modern houses, but here, larger parts of the mudbrick buildings remain in a ruinous state. Again, we are likely dealing with a street settlement. One single tower is present within the settlement, and a further six towers are dotted around the still-cultivated oasis (Schmidt *et al.* 2021).

Small hamlets

Another type of mudbrick settlement in the research area are small, loosely arranged villages or hamlets. Other than the more regular arranged settlements discussed above, they are not necessarily walled or feature other types of defence architecture such as towers. These sites include Safrat Al Khashbah, Al Likhaydir, Al Bilaydah, Al Suhayli, Al Zaydi, Al Rakhi, Al Mintarib, and Al Washhi North.

Safrat Al Khashbah is located 1 km eastwards from Al Khashbah. The settlement is spread out over two hilltops and consists of about 20 loosely arranged buildings. The mosque and the *falaj* are situated between the two hills. West of the site lies the oasis, which is out of use today and there is little modern-day construction in its surroundings. There seems to be a wall between the village and the oasis, but it is badly preserved. No towers or other defensive structures could be seen. Archaeological survey and excavation point to habitation between the 18th to 20th centuries, where the site was abandoned around the beginning of the 20th century (Biezeveld 2023).

Al Likhaydur is located next to the riverbed of the Wadi Andam. It was mentioned by Lorimer as having 60 houses and 1,000 date palms (Lorimer 1908: 78). The oasis is very elongated and currently still in use. A handful of mudbrick buildings could be recognized. One of these had a square tower made out of stone, which was well-preserved because it was made of more durable material. No other defensive structures, such as a wall, could be seen. Benkari (2017: 179) noted that settlements on flat topography would be surrounded by a town wall (*sūr*) and have fortified entrances (*ṣabāḥ*). Here, as well as some other sites in this section, this is however not the case. At this site, the authors met an Omani who explained that his grandfather used to live at the site. He explained that the site was abandoned at that time because a lack of water for the oasis. Today, the oasis is in use again because of a well.

Al Bilaydah is the largest of those loosely arranged sites, featuring several small houses on the slope of the Al Hammah mountain. It is mentioned by Scholz (1977) as an oasis where Bedouins owned or rented parts of the oasis and lived there during summer. At the highest point of the settlement, there is a partially renovated building (a staircase leading to the entrance has been reinforced with concrete). This is also the only building made out of stone, therefore it remained better preserved. Due to its position and different building material, this seems likely to have been a sheikhly house. Additionally, these houses were used to protect the inhabitants and their goods during times of war. At the bottom of the slope, next to the *falaj*, there is the Al Balidah mosque made of concrete, likely overlying the former mudbrick mosque. Next to it is the refurbished gate with the vaulted space and built-in benches typical for this architecture. It seems that there was a wall running south, but at the rest of the site, no other defensive structures were visible. Except for the still-used mosque there are no modern buildings in this settlement, but the oasis is partially under cultivation. Like at Safrat Al Khashbah, this settlement is built against the mountain to ensure their protection and confined by the oasis from their exposed lower site, which is a common strategic setting in Oman (Benkari 2017: 178).

Al Suhayli consists of few buildings situated on the foothills of the Al Hammah mountain. There are no modern buildings in its vicinity, but the surrounding fields are partially cultivated today. The architecture comprises one larger building in the east of the site, originally at least two storeys tall (Fig. 5b). This house was made of stone and mortar instead of mudbrick, which is used in the rest of the buildings. It also has defensive elements, such as shooting holes. Here, it is also assumed that we are dealing with a sheikhly house. Young (2019) mentions that a sheikh's house is usually greater in size than the other houses, and Benkari (2017) underlines the fortified appearance of these houses.

The mudbrick settlement of Al Zaydi sits on a rocky ridge in the middle of a currently cultivated oasis. Many of the mudbrick houses are refurbished or overbuilt by concrete ones and modern houses have been added surrounding the oasis. Remains of a wall are still standing at the north-eastern side of the site, indicating that it once was partially or completely walled.

Fig. 5: Al Suhayli. Brown = mudbrick houses.

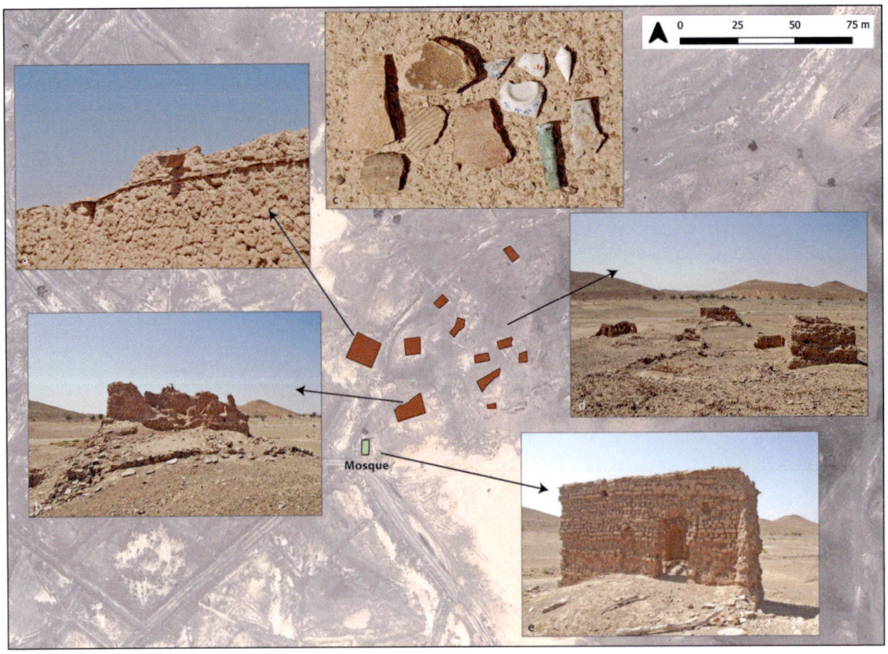

Fig. 6: Al Rakhi. Brown = mudbrick houses.

Fig. 7: Fort-like structure at Al Qabrayn.

The tower is located at the highest point of the settlement. Differently to most settlements in the research area, its tower is not maintained and half of it already collapsed.

Al Rakhi, the northernmost of those, is a small hamlet, consisting of only a dozen of scattered buildings (Fig. 6). It has been completely abandoned with no modern architecture in its surroundings and barren field systems are located to its south and south-west. In terms of structure and layout as well as preservations, it is very similar to Safrat Al Khashbah. Thus, a date for its abandonment in the late 19th or early 20th century seems likely.

Close to Al Sudayrah lies Al Mintarib. The site is located to the west of the oasis, which is still partially cultivated today. However, there are no modern houses in the surrounding. The mudbrick houses are scattered throughout the site and there is no evidence for defensive structures. In the oasis, a mosque is located. This mosque was renovated after the abandonment, which is evident from the reinforcement from concrete. Based on the archaeological finds at the site, it seems likely that it was inhabited from the 18th to the mid-20th century. This site is also mentioned by Scholz (1977) as an oasis where Bedouins owned or rented parts of the oases.

Al Mitailu lies 2.5 km southwest of Al Mintarib. It consists of a few scattered houses between a currently cultivated oasis and the modern houses of the village. The traditional houses are centred around a refurbished mosque. The majlis and a school are also located directly next to the old settlement. Lorimer mentions the settlement in his gazetteer, noting that there were 80 houses and 1,500 date palms (Lorimer 1908: 78).

The north-westernmost site is Al Washhi North, a site closely located to Al Washhi South. This site is scattered, one part is located on a hilltop, the other part on the plain. There was also a lot of slag here, indicating copper production. At this site, no remaining mudbrick architecture could be seen, there was only evidence for the stone foundations.

It thus seems likely that this site was abandoned in a period before the other sites. This is supported by the archaeological data from survey and excavation. It could be concluded that the site was inhabited during the 17th and 18th centuries, thus predating some, or most, of the sites in the research area.

Non-domestic sites

Lastly, there is the category of non-domestic sites. The only site that fits this description is Al Qabrayn (Fig. 7). This site consists of a fort-like structure, a large field system, and a handful of scattered buildings in the field system. The fort consists of two towers that are located across from each other. The towers are equipped with shooting holes and the entrance was likely on the first floor, as could be seen at other towers in the region. There are no signs of restoration or reuse at the site. Based on archaeological survey and excavation, the use of the site was likely between the late 17th and early 20th century (Biezeveld 2023).

Discussion

To better understand the settlement pattern of the mudbrick villages in the Al Mudhaybi region, there are a few patterns that seem to come forward. There appear to have been different trajectories of abandonment. There are some that were clearly abandoned after the 1970s and some that were abandoned earlier (Fig. 8). To divide this, we can make two categories: “abandoned before 1970” and “abandoned after 1970”.

There is one village that seems to have been abandoned in the 19th century, which is Al Washhi North. This abandonment could have its origin in copper mining having become no longer profitable. When Wellsted travelled from Samad Al Shan to Manah, he stopped at Kodhra (Khadra bani Daffa). Here, he mentioned that two miles to the south–southeast are copper mines, which he did not visit. He noted that the mines were still in use, but the profit was so low that it barely covered the costs (Wellsted 1838: 112–113).

There are five villages that were abandoned at the early or mid-20th century: Al Milayh, Al Mintarib, Al Qabrayn, Al Rakhi and Safrat Al Khashbah. All these villages have no evidence of modern houses in their vicinity. Three of them were classified as small hamlets, one as a compact site and one as a non-domestic site. We also see here that at three of them the oasis is currently not cultivated, and at the other two it is (partly) cultivated. At the two sites where the oasis is still (partly) in use, there are also signs of renovation; at the other sites there are no signs of this.

Fifteen sites were abandoned around or after 1970. Here, all the regional centres are attested, nine compact site settlements and five small hamlets settlements. At two of these, there is no modern construction in the site’s area, and at the rest of the sites there is modern construction at a distance or directly surrounding or even partially overbuilding the site. We also see that all oases are cultivated today. At at least ten of these sites, there is also evidence for renovation.

There are some clear differences between the sites that were abandoned before 1970 and the sites that were abandoned after 1970. First of all, there is no evidence of modern construction near the sites that were abandoned before 1970, but in almost all cases there is modern construction nearby or at the site itself for the sites that were abandoned after 1970. This is also reflected in the use of the oasis. When the site was abandoned before 1970, there seems to be no or partial use of the oasis today, and when the site was abandoned after 1970, there is always cultivation in the oasis. Additionally, more than half of the sites abandoned

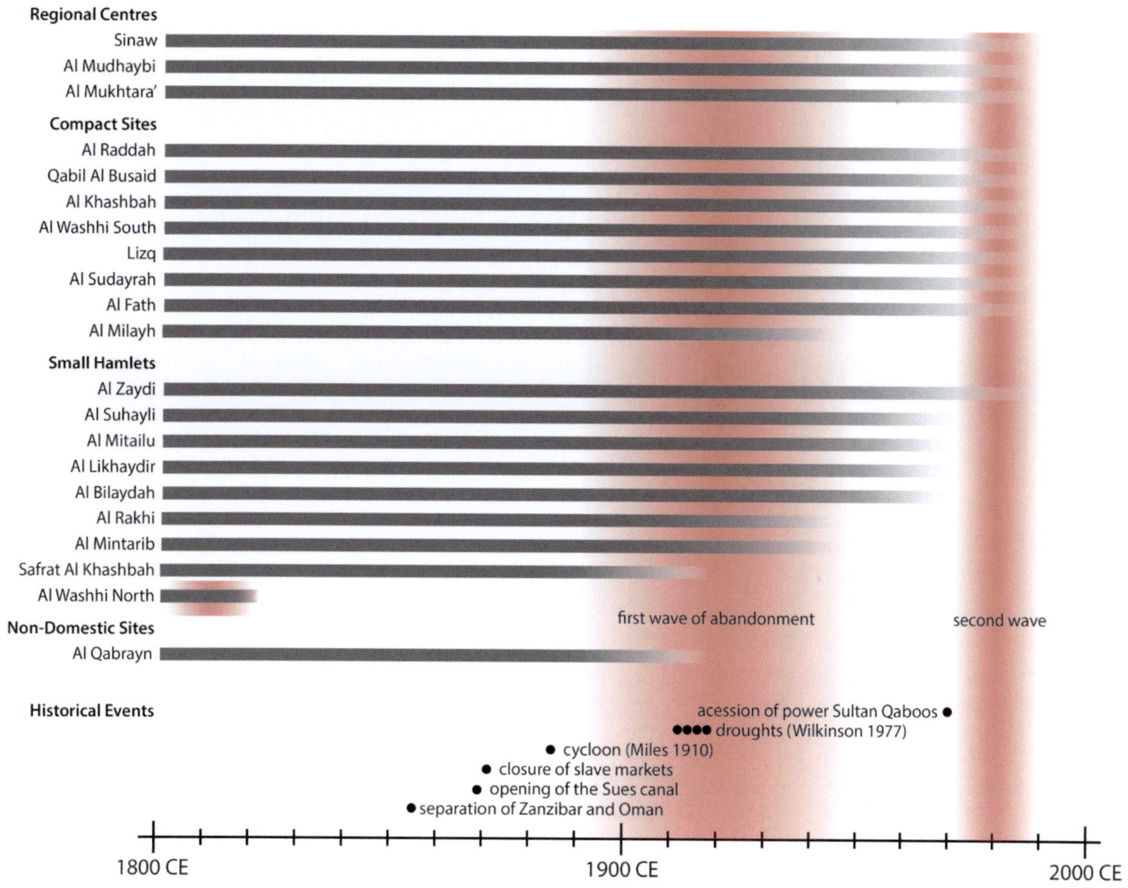

Fig. 8: Abandonment of settlements in the research area.

after 1970 have renovated parts, whereas this is less than half at the sites abandoned before 1970. These comparisons seem to indicate that when a site was abandoned before 1970, the connection to the site was weaker than when the site was abandoned after 1970.

If we relate this to the different types of sites, one can conclude that all the regional centre sites were inhabited until the 1970s. Considering the modern construction and the cultivation of the oasis, it seems evident that in these cases, the population moved from mudbrick houses to concrete houses that were built in their direct vicinity. The compact sites were almost all abandoned after 1970, except for Al Milayh, which was likely abandoned in the early or mid-20th century. In all these cases, except for Al Milayh, there is modern construction surrounding the site or partially overbuilding it, again indicating that the population likely moved from mudbrick houses to concrete houses that were built in its direct vicinity, after 1970. The small hamlets were mainly abandoned around or after 1970, but four of the sites were abandoned before this time. The sites with modern construction in the vicinity were all abandoned after 1970, again pointing to this shift from mudbrick to concrete. The sites that were abandoned before 1970 have no signs of modern construction, and in most cases, the oasis is also not cultivated today. The non-domestic site adheres to this pattern. It was abandoned before 1970, and there is no modern construction or oasis cultivation here. It thus seems that the larger the site was, the more chances it had to remain inhabited until the 1970s.

Reasons for abandonment

Most of the settlements in the study area were abandoned post-1970. This is a pattern that is visible throughout (central) Oman. In 1970, Sultan Qaboos bin Said became the Sultan of Oman and put many efforts into modernizing the country. But, in the research area, there are also six sites that were abandoned before 1970. There are various reasons for the abandonment before the modernisation processes in the 1970s. The first is a lack of natural resources, such as water, or the overexploitation of the soil. The lack of water has been mentioned as the reason for abandonment by the Omanis whom we met at Al Likhaydur. Wilkinson (1977: 195) also mentions that in the 1920s, there were droughts in central Oman, which probably led to the abandonment of many settlements in the Sharqiyah region. To check this hypothesis, the hydroclimate records from Al Hoota Cave within the Hajar Mountains were analysed (Fleitmann *et al.* 2022). These show that there was a small rise in aridity at the beginning of the 20th century, which could point to the droughts Wilkinson referred to. Just before this time, in 1885, Miles (1910: 160–161) mentioned that cyclones hit central Oman, which led to the destruction of oases and houses. Another reason for abandonment were disputes between tribes. In Sinaw, there is the example of Harat Al Barashid. Here, in the second half of the 17th century, the Al Barashid tribe from Adam and the Al Hawashim tribe from Sinaw swapped settlement quarters, because they could not live in their original settlements anymore (Ministry of Heritage and Culture 2014: 31). Also, travellers (see Miles 1910; Morris 1957; Wellsted 1838) mention that tribal unrest and disputes were common in the region.

Several political and economic events at this time should also be considered (Fig. 8). In 1832, Sayyid Said bin Sultan moved to Zanzibar, and Muscat had already lost its importance. But when he died in 1856, his two sons divided the rule between Zanzibar and Oman, with Oman being the economically weaker of the two. Many Omanis, also from central Oman, moved to Zanzibar for better economic prospects. In addition, the British government, on which Oman had become increasingly dependent, abolished the slave and arms trade; in 1873, the British forced the closure of all slave markets in Oman. In 1869, the Suez Canal was opened, allowing direct sea trade between India and Great Britain and European steamships came in, so the importance of Oman's port cities for world trade decreased significantly. There was also an increase of industrial goods, which lowered the demand for local products such as the date industry. It declined in the late 19th century and truly collapsed in the 1930s. All this also had its economic consequences for Omani trade, and as a result, also for agricultural villages. Fewer financial resources could have been put into expanding and maintaining agriculture.

Life histories of the mudbrick settlements

The general pattern of the life histories of the mudbrick settlements in the micro-region of Al Mudhaybi seems to be the following. In the 17th century, there was an increase in settlements in northern Oman (Al Jahwari 2008; Costa – Wilkinson 1987; Kennet *et al.* 2016; Mershen 2002). This was likely fuelled by the Yaʿariba Imamate, which took power in the interior of the country in 1624. Investments were made in agricultural produce through the revival of the *falaj* system (Bandyopadhyay – Mershen 2022: 7; Townsend 1977: 36). These investments continued under Al Bu Saidi rule from 1743 (Scholz 2014: 195). Most of the sites in the research area likely had their origin around this time. For only a handful of sites, a more precise origin can be suggested, which varies between the 16th to 18th centuries.

The use of the sites was mainly agricultural, which is attested for by the large field systems. From ethnographic sources, it becomes clear that Sinaw and Al Mudhaybi also acted as regional centres with a weekly market (Scholz 1977: 126). The defensive purposes of the settlements are mainly shown in regional centres, compact sites and non-domestic sites. This does not mean that small hamlets had no defences at all, but these were more often only partially walled, or maybe defensive structures were not preserved in the archaeology. At some sites, there was evidence for small-scale copper processing, and at Al Washhi North, large-scale copper processing occurred. The fact that Al Washhi North was abandoned in the 18th–19th century, whereas the sites with small-scale copper processing were abandoned in the 20th century, could indicate that around the 18th/19th century, there was a shift from larger to smaller-scale copper processing. This hypothesis should however be studied on a larger scale than the micro-region of Al Mudhaybi.

In the later 20th century, the role of the oasis towns declined and the old settlements were abandoned. Especially in the 1970s and 1980s, new concrete houses or entire new settlements were built instead (Al Jahwari 2003). But, there is also evidence that a minority of these settlements were abandoned around the 20th century, as indicated in this chapter. Reasons for this can be found in political and economic, but also climatic factors, as argued in the previous paragraph. The results from this study thus show that the abandonment patterns for traditional mudbrick villages are more diverse than sometimes suggested.

To complete the life histories approach of the settlements, we also consider their current use. There are some restoration efforts visible at the sites; these usually concern the mosque or a tower and, in some cases, sheikhly house(s). Additionally, most of the sites that were completely abandoned and that had no modern houses in the neighbourhood were considered to be a nice location for a day-trip and a picnic. At the sites where there is no current cultivation of the oasis, there are also no signs of renovation. At the sites where there are no modern houses, there is only evidence for renovation when the oasis is (partly) cultivated. When a site is abandoned, the type of site does not seem to play a role in whether or not there were renovation efforts. Of all the types and from all the different abandonment dates, there are examples of sites where no renovation is present.

Conclusion

This chapter aimed to reconstruct the life histories of the mudbrick settlements in the micro-region of Al Mudhaybi. Here, a total of 21 settlements were recorded through remote sensing. These settlements were visited in 2022 by the authors, and five of these were investigated in more detail in the dissertation of Biezeveld (2023). The settlements were evaluated to learn more about the foundation, use, and abandonment, as well as reuse and incorporation into the modern settlement pattern. For the Al Mudhaybi area, we can conclude that an increase in settlement in the 17th century can be linked to the Yaʿariba Imamate, which took control of inland and coastal Oman in 1624. The Yaʿariba invested in the agricultural expansion in the interior of Oman, which can be seen in the main function of the settlements in the region. All, except one, are linked to an oasis, which is in most cases still partly cultivated today. There is also evidence for copper processing in the area, and defensive structures occur often. Most settlements were abandoned around or after 1970, when Sultan Qaboos bin Said modernized the country. Some settlements were abandoned earlier, likely due to climatic, political or economic reasons. At some of the settlements, restoration efforts could be seen, but these were mainly focussed on religious or defensive structures. What comes forward from this study is that in contrast to many of the previously published sites, we focus not just on one site in particular, but try and understand the life histories and settlement pattern of a whole region. This allowed us to focus on various settlement functions, reasons for abandonment, and forms of reuse that were not published before. From this, we can conclude that there is a larger variability than is suggested from previous studies, with regard to reasons of abandonment of the sites, as well as reuse of the sites. This emphasizes the need to include a more diverse set of approaches and case studies when studying the mudbrick settlements of (central) Oman. The past consensus on the foundation and abandonment of the settlements has been shown to not be true for all Late Islamic settlements in Oman. Additionally, new alternative forms of reuse at the abandoned sites are proposed in this study.

References

Al Jahwari, N. S. 2003
Ancient quarters in Oman: An urgency in the archaeology of Oman, in: Ministry of Heritage and Culture – UNESCO World Heritage Centre (eds), *Proceedings Regional Seminar on the Conservation of Earthen Structures in the Arab Countries*, Muscat, 35–44.

Al Jahwari, N. S. 2008
Settlement patterns, development and cultural change in Northern Oman Peninsula: a multi-tiered approach to the analysis of long-term settlement trends [PhD Dissertation, Durham University].

Al Ghafri, A. 2018
Overview about the aflaj of Oman [paper presented at the International Symposium of Khattaras and Aflaj].

Appadurai, A. (ed.) 1986
The social life of things: Commodities in cultural perspective, Cambridge.

Bandyopadhyay, S. – Mershen, B. 2022
Falaj communities in Oman: A case for local governance? Ibāḍī legal rulings and spatial and ethnohistorical observations, *Journal of Material Cultures in the Muslim World* 3/1, 6–47. DOI:10.1163/26666286-12340028

Bandyopadhyay, S. – Sibley, M. 2003
The distinctive typology of central Omani mosques: its nature and antecedents, *Proceedings of the Seminar for Arabian Studies* 33, 99–116.

Benkari, N. 2017
The defensive vernacular settlements in Oman, a contextual study, *International Journal of Heritage Architecture* 1/2, 175–184. DOI:10.2495/ha-v1-n2-175-184

Biezeveld, I. 2022
Re(dis)covering the recent: Surveying settlements and society in central Oman from the 17th to the 20th centuries, *Arabian Archaeology and Epigraphy* 34, 107–121. DOI:10.1111/AAE.12225

Biezeveld, I. 2023
The abandoned villages of central Oman: Use and reuse of Late Islamic settlements (1650-1970 CE) in the Al Mudhaybi region [unpublished PhD thesis, Goethe University Frankfurt].

Bonnenfant, P. – Bonnenfant, G. – Al Harthi, S. 1977
Architecture and social history at Mudayrib, *The Journal of Oman Studies* 3, 107–136.

Costa, P. M. – Wilkinson, T. J. 1987
The hinterland of Sohar. Archaeological surveys and excavations within the region of an Omani seafaring city, The Journal of Oman Studies 9.

Damluji, S. S. 1998
The architecture of Oman, Reading.

Döpper, S. 2019
Spätbronzezeitliche Keramik aus dem Königspalast von Qaṭna und eine vergleichende Betrachtung zeitgleicher Keramikassemblagen Westsyriens und der Levante, Qatna Studien 7, Wiesbaden.

Döpper, S. 2022a
Survey methods and biases in the Al-Mudhaybi Regional Survey, Sultanate of Oman, *Arabian Archaeology and Epigraphy*, 29–50. DOI: 10.1111/aae.12224

Döpper, S. 2022b
Walk the Line: The 2020 field season of the Al-Mudhaybi Regional Survey, *Proceedings of the Seminar for Arabian Studies* 51, 157–167.

Döpper, S. 2023
Mud-brick villages and open-air mosques: The Late Islamic landscape of the Al-Mudhaybi Region in central Oman, in: N. Marchetti – F. Cavaliere – E. Cirelli, C. D'Orazio – G. Giacosa – M. Guidetti – E. Mariani (eds), *Proceedings of the 12th International Congress on the Archaeology of the Ancient Near East, 06-09 April 2021, Bologna*, Wiesbaden, 945–956.

Döpper, S. – Schmidt, C. 2020
Nothing but tombs and towers? Results of the Al-Mudhaybi Regional Survey 2019, *Proceedings of the Seminar for Arabian Studies* 50, 157–169.

Gaube, H. – Gangler, A. 2012
Transformation processes in oasis settlements of Oman, Muscat.

Fleitmann, D. – Haldon, J. – Bradley, R. S. – Burns, S. J. – Cheng, H. – Lawrence Edwards, R. – Raible, C. C. – Jacobson, M. – Matter, A. 2022
Droughts and societal change: The environmental context for the emergence of Islam in late Antique Arabia, *Science 376*, 1317–1321.

Gerritsen, F. 1999
To build and to abandon: The cultural biography of late prehistoric houses and farmsteads in the southern Netherlands, *Archaeological Dialogues* 6/2, 78–97. DOI: 10.1017/S1380203800001410

Gosden, C. – Marshall, Y. 1999
The cultural biography of objects, *World Archaeology* 31/2, 169–178.

Grey, T. 2011
Late trade wares on the Arabian shores: 18th- to 20th-century imported fineware ceramics from excavated sites on the southern Persian (Arabian) Gulf coast, *Post-Medieval Archaeology* 4/2, 350–373. DOI: 10.1179/174581311X13135030529557

Hughes-Thomas, R. (ed.) 1856
Arabian Gulf Intelligence. Selections from the records of the Bombay Government. New series, no. XXIV, concerning Arabia, Bahrain, Kuwait, Muscat and Oman, Qatar, United Arab Emirates and the Islands of the Gulf, Bombay.

Holtorf, C. 2002
Notes on the life history of a pot sherd, *Journal of Material Culture* 7/1, 49–71. DOI:10.1177/1359183502007001305

Kennet, D. – Deadman, W. M. – Al Jahwari, N. S. 2016
The Rustaq-Batinah Archaeological Survey, *Proceedings of the Seminar for Arabian Studies* 46, 155–168.

Kopytoff, I. 1986
The cultural biography of things: Commoditization as process, in: A. Appadurai (ed.), *The social life of things: Commodities in cultural perspective*, Cambridge, 64–92. DOI:10.1017/CBO9780511819582.004

Landen, R. G. 1967
Oman since 1856. Disruptive modernization in a traditional society, Princeton.

Lorimer, J. G. 1908
Gazetteer of the Persian Gulf, Oman, and Central Arabia 2.

Mershen, B. 2002
"Let the water run back". Archaeological and ethnohistorical observations from Wadi Fanjah / Wadi al-Khod, Oman: the case of a failed 18th/19th century agro-economic enterprise, *Proceedings of the Seminar for Arabian Studies* 32, 99–116.

Miles, S. B. 1896
Journal of an excursion in Oman, in South-East Arabia, *The Geographical Journal* 7/5, 522–537.

Miles, S. B. 1910
On the border of the great desert: A journey in Oman, *The Geographical Journal* 36/2, 159–178.

Miles, S. B. 1919
The countries and tribes of the Persian Gulf, London.

Ministry of Heritage and Culture 2014
Sinaw: Harat al-Burashdi & Harat al-Suwawfah. Documentation and heritage management plan, Muscat.

Ministry of Tourism 2016
Al-Hamra: Misfat al-Abriyin. Tourism development plan, Muscat.

Morris, J. 1957
Sultan in Oman. Venture into the Middle East, New York.

Overholtzer, L. – Stoner, W. D. 2011
Merging the social and the material: Life histories of ancient mementos from central Mexico, *Journal of Social Archaeology* 11/2, 171–193. DOI:10.1177/1469605311399072

Power, T. 2015
A first ceramic chronology for the Late Islamic Arabian Gulf, *Journal of Islamic Archaeology* 2/1, 1–33. DOI:10.1558/jia.v2i1.27011

Reniere, S. – de Clercq, W. 2018
Gallo-Roman whetstone building deposits. The cultural biography of the domestic sphere in northern Gaul, *Journal of Anthropological Archaeology* 51, 67–76. DOI: 10.1016/j.jaa.2018.05.006

Samson, R. (ed.) 1990
The social archaeology of houses, Edinburgh.

Schiffer, M. B. 1972
Archaeological context and systemic context, *American Antiquity* 37/2, 156–165. DOI: 10.2307/278203

Schmidt, C. – Döpper, S. – Kluge, J. – Petrella, S. – Ochs, U. – Kirchhoff, N. – Maier, S. – Walter, M. 2021
Die Entstehung komplexer Siedlungen im Zentraloman. Archäologische Untersuchungen zur Siedlungsgeschichte von Al-Khashbah, Oxford.

Scholz, F. 1977
Die beduinischen Stämme im östlichen Inner-Oman und ihr Regional-Mobilitäts-Verhalten, *Sociologus* 27/2, 97–133.

Scholz, F. 1984
Falaj-Oasen in Sharqiya, Inner-Oman, *Die Erde* 115, 273–294.

Scholz, F. 2014
Muscat: Then and now, Muscat.

Stiffe, A. W. 1897
Ancient trading centres of the Persian Gulf: IV Maskat, *The Geographical Journal* 10/6, 608–618.

Townsend, J. 1977
Oman: The making of the modern state, London.

Wellsted, J. R. 1838
Travels in Arabia I, London.

Wilkinson, J. C. 1977
Water and tribal settlement in South-East Arabia. A study of the aflaj of Oman, Oxford.

Young, R. 2019
Historical archaeology and heritage in the Middle East, London.

Živković, J. – Power, T. – Georgakopoulou, M. – Carvajal López, J. C. 2019
Defining new technological traditions of Late Islamic Arabia: a view on Bahlā Ware from al-Ain (UAE) and the lead-barium glaze production, *Archaeological and Anthropological Sciences* 11/9, 4697–4709. DOI: 10.1007/S12520-019-00807-6/TABLES/5

Memory and Belonging in the Bat Oasis, Oman

Ruth Young, with a contribution by Alasdair Brooks

Introduction

The largely derelict mudbrick buildings that make up the oasis or village of Bat in central Oman are tangible reminders of ways of life that characterised rural, interior Oman for centuries until Sultan Qaboos' accession to the throne in 1970. Sultan Qaboos' key aims early in his reign included the modernisation, westernisation, and unification of his country (Valeri 2009). Shifting from the use of mudbrick as the main domestic building material to concrete was a major signifier of this move towards modernity right across Oman, but many mudbrick settlements were simply left in place beside the new settlements rather than being destroyed.

In 2012 the "Bat Oasis Historical Archaeology Project" was developed, with the key aims of learning more about the significance of the mudbrick to former inhabitants, and understanding the importance of these buildings and remains of the earlier village as place, and in memory, and about the intersection of place and memory (Young *et al.* 2018). Carrying out building analysis, excavation and interviews as part of a field project in Bat allowed the project team to develop understandings of life in rural villages prior to the 1970s, which demonstrated how important the extant mudbrick remains are in terms of memory and belonging. Using place as an analytical framework and Bat as a case study, this chapter explores ways in which abandoned, derelict structures provide a strong anchor (and prompt) for individual and social memory, as well as contributing to a sense of belonging for those who formerly lived in them.

This chapter draws on results from the "Bat Oasis Historical Archaeology Project" carried out between 2012 and 2016. The project explored the mudbrick village of Bat through archaeological planning, excavations, building analyses, and interviews with former inhabitants, in order to develop multiple understandings of the meanings of the mudbrick structures and their role in holding and providing memories.

Bat – background

The settlement of Bat is located in the interior of Oman, on the western side of the Al Hajar mountains that separate the interior from the coast. Throughout most of the 20th century up to the 1970s the Sultanate of Muscat and Oman was characterised as a very closed,

in: S. Döpper – B. Mershen – J. Kanditt – I. Biezeveld – T. Schmidt-Lux (eds) 2025, *Mudbrick Settlements of the Oman Peninsula. Inhabited – Abandoned – Re(dis)covered*, Leiden: Sidestone Press, 33–50.

traditional country. The country was basically divided into two main operating spheres: Muscat and the coast were ruled by a secular leader, while the interior (including the desert and the mountain chain separating the interior from the coast) formed Oman, which was ruled by an Islamic (Ibadi) Imamate (Allen 1987: 9; Owtram 2004: 43). The settled nature of much of Oman's population (although there has always been a sizeable mobile, or Bedou minority (Chatty 2013)) means it has been very different to the rest of the Arabian Peninsula, which has led to a singular understanding and use of place. This pattern of permanent settlements was critical also in allowing the development of the Imamate, which is unique in Islam and was very much rooted in place, in the interior where particular historical figures were located, and particular political systems made it possible. Although the power of the Imamate was considerably curbed in the early 20th century through actions such as the Seeb Agreement (1920), dissatisfaction with the secular leadership periodically resulted in rebellions from the interior, including the Tanuf rebellion of the mid-1950s. It was only in the 1970s with the accession of Sultan Qaboos bin Said to the throne that the country was fully and effectively united to become modern Oman, and the Imamate effectively suppressed (Clark 2008: 235; Owtram 2004; Valieri 2009).

Security was a major issue in the country for centuries, and was arguably a factor in the success or otherwise of the Imamate and Imamate cycle. Feuding between tribes was a part of life up until the 1970s, and this is evidenced through the multiple mudbrick fortifications and towers that are an integral part of the built landscape of the mudbrick settlements of Oman (Bandyopadhyay 2011; Graz 1982: 72; Wellsted 1978 (1838)). Security, or rather insecurity, was something noted by various travellers to Oman, including these 19th century accounts from travels in interior Oman, for example from a British officer in the Indian Navy: "The principal tribes were now at feud, a single individual was rarely met with beyond the precincts of the villages, nor was it without some precaution that our own party proceeded" (Wellsted 1978 (1838): 51). In the absence of a strong central leadership providing security, protection for settlements such as Bat came from the Sheikh, who not only maintained the central fortified castle or *ḥusn*, but also coordinated the lookout systems and armed forces to protect people and property during conflict.

Against a long-term background of dissent from the Imamate and its supporters, security concerns, and slowly increasing contact with the "outside" world, i.e. that beyond Oman, there was significant growing opposition to Sultan Said, and on 23 July 1970 he was deposed. The new Sultan Qaboos bin Taimur Al Said faced many political, economic, and social issues in the fractured country he inherited in the middle of 1970 (Valeri 2009). In direct opposition to his father's resolve to keep Oman shielded from westerners and western developments, Qaboos began a determined move to modernise and westernise his country, his renaissance or *nahḍa*, which has impacted on virtually all aspects of life in the intervening 50 years, and nowhere more so than mudbrick houses and villages. One of the major changes evident under Sultan Qaboos was the move from mudbrick houses into newly built concrete block houses (Al Jahwari 2006). Homes are perhaps one of the most intimate places in most peoples' lives, tied up with memory, identity, belonging, and (certainly in Omani villages), core to family structures and village social structures.

Bat comprises a contemporary settlement adjacent to a UNESCO World Heritage (WH) site "The Archaeological sites of Bat, Al Khutm and Al Ayn" (UNESCO 2023). The name "Bat" refers to both the recently abandoned (from the 1980s to the early 2000s) mudbrick structures and their concrete replacements (i.e. the settlement), and the Bronze Age tombs, towers, and other traces of prehistoric activity such as water management features that contribute to the WH site. The Bat WH site is incredibly important in terms of understandings of prehistory and is described thus: “The protohistoric site of Bat lies near a palm grove in the interior of the Sultanate of Oman. Together with the neighbouring sites, it forms the most complete collection of settlements and necropolises from the 3rd millennium B.C. in the world” (UNESCO 2023). Archaeological projects have been carried out at the Bat WH sites exploring the prehistoric archaeological remains for several decades, most recently by an American team from Penn Museum (Thornton *et al.* 2016). The archaeological importance of the prehistoric features and landscape meant that all scholarly attention was focused on this aspect of Bat, with the much more recent mudbrick remains neglected. Academics working in other parts of Bat recognised the value of studying the mudbrick via their own disciplines (e.g. Al Jahwari 2006; Bandyopadhyay 2011), but until the 2012 project was set up, there had been no sustained attempt to study a mudbrick village as an archaeological site. In recent years, however, the work by Biezeveld (2022) and the “Lost Cities Project” has also demonstrated very clearly that different research questions and themes can be effectively explored using archaeological approaches in the abandoned mudbrick settlements of Oman.

Mudbrick at Bat

Our focus on mudbrick structures in Bat included planning individual houses (as well as the whole village), carrying out building analysis and recording, excavating within rooms in different houses, analysing the artefacts and features recovered during excavation, and carrying out interviews with people who had lived in these mudbrick houses before moving to new concrete houses. We also had site visits with these informants, where they talked about the use of different rooms in houses, and identified the different sorts of activities that would have taken place there.

Like most mudbrick villages and towns in Oman, at the centre of Bat is a mudbrick *ḥusn* or castle, the Husn Al Wardi, which is situated on the highest point of land in Bat. The *ḥusn* has not been demolished, although parts of it have been severely eroded since 2015, and it still sits at the heart of the old settlement. The largest house in the village belonged to the sheikh, and was an imposing mudbrick structure right next to the *ḥusn*, and the mudbrick house is still standing, with the new concrete house beside it. There are also a number of Bronze Age towers in the oasis (see Fig. 1); these Bronze Age towers are an important part of the WH site of Bat and also play a role in the memory and place of the mudbrick settlement, discussed further below.

In reality it is incorrect to say that all of the mudbrick buildings of the Bat oasis or village are abandoned. While many of the mudbrick houses, civic buildings and agricultural structures that were part of Bat have been destroyed (either cleared for expanding agriculture, the building of new houses, or through neglect and weathering), and many that are still standing are no longer used for their original purposes, a number of mudbrick structures have been adapted for different uses. Currently, the greatest concentration of mudbrick houses still standing lies to the south east of the *ḥusn*. Elsewhere there is a mix of mudbrick and new concrete buildings in other parts of the village (Fig. 2), while the highest concentration of concrete houses and buildings is found to the west of the *ḥusn*, along the main tarmac road linking Bat to Al Dariz and then on to Ibri. There are also a number of mudbrick farmhouses in the areas around the edge of the village. The rest of

Fig. 1: Bat mudbrick and Husn Al Wardi.

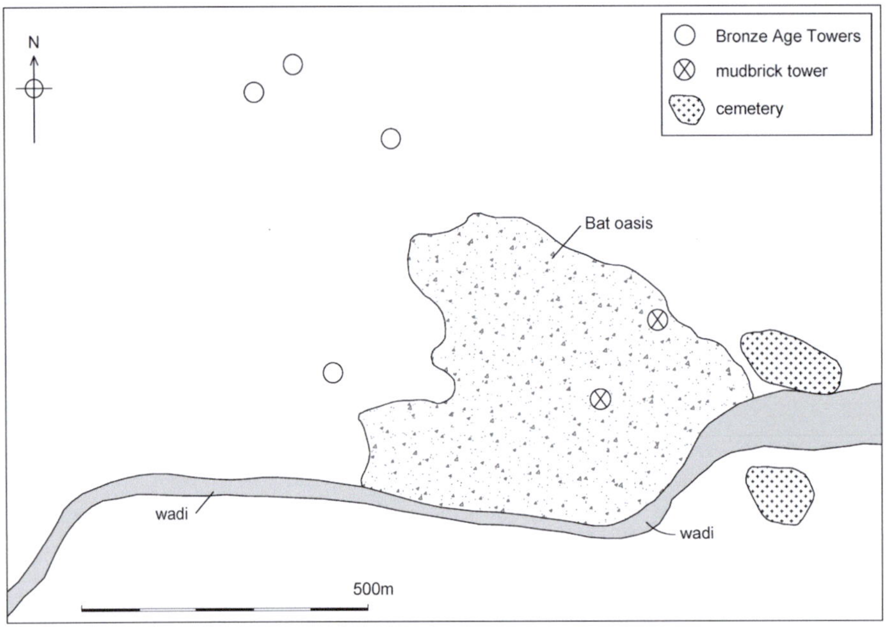

Fig. 2: Location of Bronze Age towers and mudbrick towers in and around Bat oasis.

Fig. 3: Bat mudbrick below Husn Al Wardi.

Fig. 4: Mudbrick and concrete (sheikh's house).

the oasis has mudbrick mosques, some shops, many houses, and mudbrick field walls, all in different stages of repair and decline. While some parts of the mudbrick village have been abandoned entirely, in other places concrete houses and structures have been built in between mudbrick, or replacing mudbrick and this results in a sort of interleaving of mudbrick and concrete (Fig. 3 and Fig. 4).

That the mudbrick has been left to stand and decay at its own rate in many places across Oman rather than being demolished is important for memory and maintaining physical links to the past. While HM Sultan Qaboos wanted his country and citizens to be modern and forward looking, removing these reminders and memories of past lifeways was clearly not a priority. The building of the new concrete settlement next to the mudbrick occurred in many places such as Ibri, Birkat Al Mawz, Miskin, Hamra, Adam, and Tanuf for example. The mudbrick settlements of these towns and villages remained largely intact as the new concrete houses, shops, mosques, public buildings and so forth were created from scratch as whole new settlements right next to them. The mudbrick settlements are now used for various informal activities, and act as the setting for such things as children's games, private places for migrant workers to gather, places for visitors to explore. In other places such as Bat the mudbrick structures are mixed in with newer concrete structures, and the survival of mudbrick is less complete. This interleaving of the mudbrick and concrete may well be due to multiple factors, including the convenience of keeping mudbrick and incorporating walls in newer structures rather than knocking it down and clearing it away. That some mudbrick buildings have been cleared away fully in Bat to make way for new houses may also be due to a desire to remain close to the *ḥusn*; this is not evident in the other villages noted above, and presents a different physical understanding of the remains of the past.

Results

Interviews

People tell stories about place, to themselves and to others, as ways of finding meaning and their place in the world, and this is something that was very evident in our interviews. We carried out formal interviews with 12 people and informal discussions and site visits with a further 5 people (Young *et al.* 2018). We spoke to both men and women ranging in ages from early 30s to 80s, and the formal interviews were conducted either in their own houses and compounds or while seated in the mudbrick area of Bat below the *ḥusn*, depending on their preference. Many of those interviewed also walked with us around the mudbrick areas and buildings talking about where they had lived, where others had lived, what specific buildings and rooms had been used for. Drawing directly on memories, our interviewees would often tell stories around events that had happened in the villages, even within particular spaces and buildings, and these stories not only helped them to share aspects of life in the villages with us, but also allows them to define their own place within both the physical and social structures of the villages (Young 2019).

In these interviews "mudbrick" often became a shorthand way of referring to particular aspects of the past that are now believed to be lost. These lost things included neighbourliness, a sense of community and caring, and a general "looking out for one another". Living in mudbrick was very closely linked to a now lost sense of community. Further, interviewees almost always went on to mourn the loss of these social interactions as a result of living in the separateness of concrete houses (Young 2019). This loss may be as much a result of family fragmentation through political and economic changes that have led to greater urbanisation and separation into nuclear rather than extended families, but interviewees were able to use the buildings – the mudbrick – to represent the major social changes that had occurred in the last 40–50 years. Mudbrick was also a place where their parents, grandparents and other now dead family members had lived, and this invested the mudbrick with strong and specific memories of people, activities, events, and time.

This nostalgia for aspects of the past did not mean that our interviewees were simply telling us about an idealised version of life in mudbrick. Some of these former occupants also had a sharp sense of problems with mudbrick houses which tended to be about convenience and comfort rather than the wider social and economic structures. Tellingly, a sense of loss for the community and sociability of living in mudbrick and a sense of nostalgia around the lost ways of life did not preclude the appreciation of indoor kitchens, plumbing, and electricity. Although, one older woman we interviewed did say that she missed the wooden pegs that had protruded from the walls of the kitchen in her mudbrick house; we had gone with her to look at her old family home, and some of walls were still standing with wooden pegs *in situ* in many walls of different rooms. It seemed that a fitted modern kitchen was not entirely convenient and satisfactory in all ways. The importance of indoor bathrooms and toilets for women and girls was also stressed in terms of privacy and safety in concrete houses, compared to mudbrick (Young *et al.* 2018; Young 2019).

Despite the recognition of drawbacks around mudbrick it is undeniably special in the minds of those who used to live in it; it is perceived very much as a place of belonging through family ties, and is the place where there was a "true" sense of community. The people we interviewed strongly and uniformly associated the mudbrick structures and mudbrick village with a community that cared about its members and provided strong support. The ruined mudbrick structures in evidence today are the tangible link to this past emotion and understanding, and provide a sense of belonging. At least three of our interviewees said that the mudbrick village was so important to them, that it appeared in their dreams (Young 2019). The mudbrick permits older people to remember and reminisce, and allows nostalgia; the structures, the place are very powerful, tangible repositories of both memory and belonging. Mudbrick is a very clear representation of the past, and many of our interviewees thought it important that this be saved for the next generation, so they did not lose a knowledge of where they came from.

Excavations

Analysis of the features uncovered during excavations, along with the artefacts recovered (see section below), provides an opportunity to explore memory and place through material culture rather than direct, recent accounts. We excavated within three houses plus one shop, and then within the *ḥusn*, opening a total of 12 trenches. Our trenches were relatively small (1 m × 2 m maximum), which was necessary in order not to undermine or disturb standing walls and permission was acquired from current landowners. Two of the houses were located in the concentration of mudbrick buildings to the east of the *ḥusn* (see Fig. 5), and one was a detached farmhouse further away from the *ḥusn* on its own in the oasis. We were able to interview the former owner of "Rashid's House" (being Rashid bin Saif Al Jassassi himself) and someone who had lived next door to the "Camel Driver's House" (their own house having been demolished some years earlier). We were not able to interview anyone who had lived in the farmhouse. A small shop was an integral part of Rashid's House

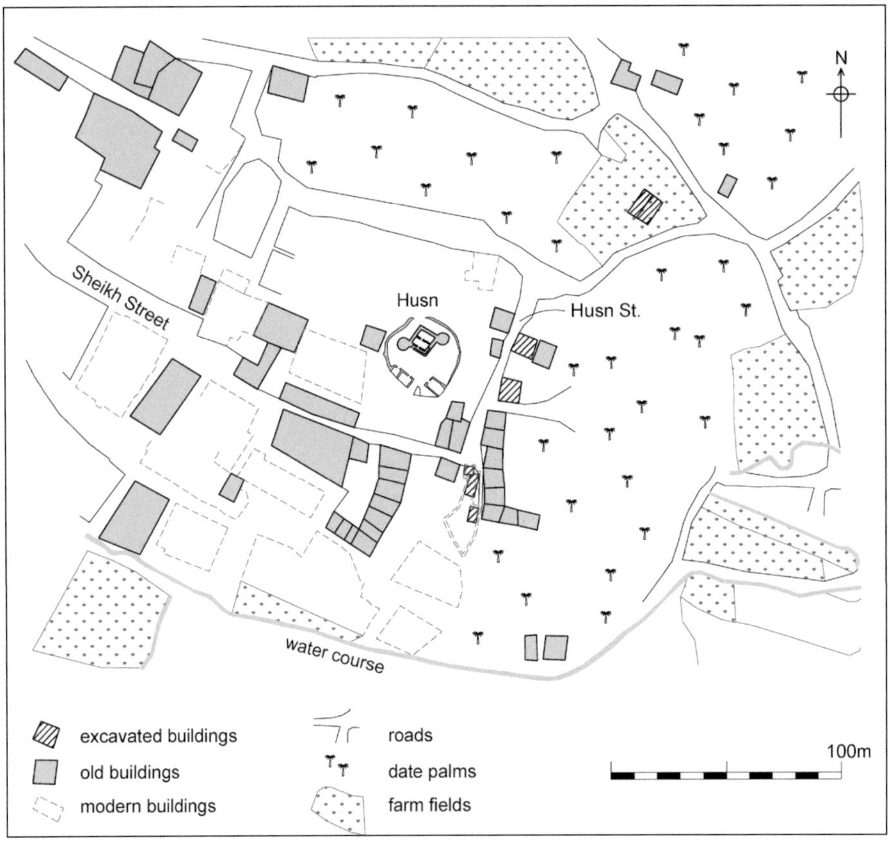

Fig. 5: Location of excavations in Bat Oasis.

and run by his family, although it had a separate entrance and could only be accessed from the street, and not from the house itself (Young *et al.* 2018).

From the layers relating to the historical (or pre-modern period, i.e., *in situ* occupation layers up to the 1970s (or 1950s – see below in the Artefacts Report for further discussion of dating of layers) we found a range of artefacts such as date honey making pots in the kitchen, and also features such as hearths, wooden posts for coffee grinding, and postholes for posts for tethering animals, in line with the function of the room as discussed during interviews and site visits. Once below the historical layers, we either came down onto natural soil very quickly, or onto pre-historic layers and features very quickly, depending on the location of the houses. In the houses close to the castle, that is, the oldest part of the village, we came down onto prehistoric material – artefacts and features. Under the earliest historic floor in the store room of Rashid's house we came down in one end of the trench onto a layer with Iron Age pottery including possible iron working mould fragments, and then in the other end of the trench directly onto the top of a Bronze Age stone wall (Young *et al.* 2018).

Directly below the lowest pre-modern or historical layer in the living room of the same house we came down onto a single burial – there were no artefacts associated with the skeleton, and we were unable to get a radiocarbon date estimate because the bones were too badly degraded – the common situation with human burials in this region. Although the skeleton was not exactly facing Makkah, it was partially turned on one side to face

Fig. 6: Umm an-Nar tomb at Bat reconstructed from original stone blocks.

east (Young *et al.* 2018). Our archaeological representative decided it was not an Islamic burial so we could lift it, but without direct dates on the bones or dateable artefacts it could be any date from c. 150 years old (the approximate date we were given for great-grandparents building their house in this area) to Bronze Age (being the earliest known activity here to date).

We also recorded an interesting set of stone blocks in the wall of one of the mudbrick houses just below the castle. These blocks have been identified as stones from an Umm an-Nar Bronze Age period tomb dated to c. 2600–2000 BCE (see Fig. 6 and Fig. 7). This is the only example of this re-use of stone from the tombs that we have noted across the village, and these distinctive blocks certainly do not provide any structural purpose in the building, so would have been included because they were pleasing, and made the building distinctive, and possibly because they created a link to the features in the surrounding landscape, and possibly even to the past.

At this point in thinking through memory and place it is worth returning to the Bronze Age towers of Bat and their role in the mudbrick village. There are some seven Bronze Age towers around Bat that have fascinated archaeologists for many years, and of course play a major role in the WH listing. The presence of a Bronze Age tower under the mudbrick castle had been speculated on the basis of the large stone blocks in the same style and circular formation as the towers being visible in the exterior profile (see Fig. 9), although these might of course have been re-used from other towers and transported here for use in the building of the *ḥusn* (Young 2019).

In order to find out more about this putative Bronze Age tower we also carried out excavation between the outer wall of the *ḥusn* and the tower over the area of

Fig. 7: Umm an-Nar blocks in mudbrick house.

possible Bronze Age blocks identified in *ḥusn* profile. We uncovered a series of historical period floors, and under the historical layers in this tower trench, we came down onto a Bronze Age wall with construction identical to that recorded inside other towers that had been excavated, thus helping to confirm this underlying structure as a Bronze Age tower. We were also able to obtain charcoal samples for dating from the layer overlaying the wall, and the results indicate that the castle was first established here in the 14th century, in line with other early construction estimates from other castles in the region (Young 2019).

Fig. 8: Bronze Age tower under mudbrick *ḥusn*.

This link between the recent past (i.e., the occupation and activity here of the last few centuries), and the remains of a much deeper past are interesting and important in terms of analysing place and memory here. This Bronze Age tower (that is, the one under the present mudbrick *ḥusn*) was built on the highest piece of land in the area, in a bend in the wadi. The lack of accumulated material between the top of the Bronze Age wall and the earliest historic period layer of the current mudbrick *ḥusn* suggests that at least some structural elements would have been visible on the surface in the 14th century (Young 2019). Also, given the lack of accumulation between the lowest historical layer in the store-room of Rashid's House and the top of the Bronze Age wall directly underneath it, it is highly likely that this wall would have been visible on the surface when the house location was selected. Whether the builders of the earliest version of the *ḥusn* in Bat, and of the first houses below it, were aware of the actual time depth of the earlier occupation remains is not known, and perhaps is not terribly important (Young *et al.* 2018). Arguably the important issue here is that these earlier structures were part of the landscape being settled, part of the place that was being occupied and shaped into the needs of those building here from the 14th century onwards. While understanding of the academic significance and value of the prehistoric landscape of Bat is limited among current occupants, there is an awareness of these earlier remains. How people choose to engage with the wider prehistoric landscape varies, but there is strong positive engagement with the more recent mudbrick landscape, and that encompasses much older remains.

Artefacts (from the Artefacts Report by Alasdair Brooks)

The artefacts and the contexts they came from fall into two main groups: a lower (earlier) group, and a higher (later) group. The lower, earlier historical (pre-modern) layers or contexts and the accompanying artefact signature consist almost exclusively of bone, shell, and the local coarse glazed earthenwares known as Bahla or Kunj ware, which was widespread right across large parts of the Arabian peninsula and southern Iran. Rob Carter (2011) describes this ware type as dying out in the late 19th to early 20th century, hypothesising that it is replaced by imports of European whitewares and cheap Chinese porcelain. The only item in these historical contexts that is clearly identifiable as an import is a single fragment of Chinese porcelain, and the only artefact in the historical contexts with a solid diagnostic date is a coin of Sultan Faisal bin Turki (r. 1888–1913), the great-grandfather of Sultan Qaboos.

The upper, more recent modern layers contain 20th century artefacts, notably plastic and modern machine-made bottle glass. Imported items and objects with international brand names associated with 20th century globalised capitalism are common in these layers, which clearly date to the later decades of the century. For example, relevant artefacts include (though are not limited to) complete bottles of RC Cola and Orange Crush with Arabic transliterations of the soft drinks' English names (كولا; ارسي كراش) (see Fig. 9).

Each assemblage group at Bat shows what we are calling a very clear "*Nahḍa* or Renaissance horizon". Either a context is dominated by modern artefacts such as plastic and modern bottle glass deeming it "post-Renaissance", or it is a "pre-Renaissance" context with no (or virtually no) imported materials at all. This "Renaissance horizon" also has broader implications in terms of the impacts of political and economic changes at Bat. The Bat assemblages indicate an almost total lack of material engagement between the oasis and the outside world prior to the latter half of the 20th century (Young *et al.* 2018). While we see European ceramics appearing at sites across the wider region from 1870 onwards, this is just not happening at Bat.

The distinctive change from local artefacts to imported artefacts can be understood in the light of the two key events in the second half of the 20th century that together meant Oman was transformed politically, socially, and economically: the cessation of the Ibadi Imamate following events at Tanuf in the 1950s, and the accession of HM Sultan Qaboos and the "Renaissance" or *nahḍa* of Oman in the 1970s (Valeri 2009: 130–131). At present, it is not possible to prove whether the arrival of external "modern" globalised material culture is a post-1950s or post-1970s phenomenon. While 20 years is a small gap in archaeological terms, it is crucial in deciding whether the transformation in consumption is a consequence of the collapse of the Imamate in the 1950s or the Renaissance instituted by Sultan Qaboos in the 1970s, or whether it may be the result of men from Bat travelling outside Oman for work and returning with manufactured goods. Further research on the brand names and logos on the plastic and glass artefacts may help to settle this issue.

While the study of what are often called "European trade wares" in local contexts is still developing in the region, late 19th- and early 20th-century imported ceramics are widespread and recurring (though not necessarily always common) features of assemblages in both the United Arab Emirates and Qatar (Carter 2011; Grey 2011; Sasaki – Sasaki 2012; Brooks 2014; Brooks – Young 2016: 29–30). While a date range of c. 1870–c. 1930 has been identified for the majority of these on the basis of makers marks on Dutch ceramics found in both Qatar and the UAE, there are hints that the first introduction of British ceramics in the region may have occurred as early as the General Maritime Treaty of 1820 (Brooks 2014: 7–8). The Faisal bin Turki coin from

Fig. 9: Soda bottles from post-Renaissance context.

Bat suggests that at least some of the Bat pre-Renaissance contexts are from the period where these European ceramics are most common in the Gulf, yet they are totally absent from Bat. Further research will no doubt allow further exploration of these potentially significant themes.

Place, belonging and memory

Place as a concept is widely understood as spaces that have not only had some form of human intervention, but are made meaningful by people through their actions within place, and by their beliefs (Cresswell 2015: 2; Massey 2002: 1994). Just as people impact on places, places impact on people as this is a recursive relationship. The connections of place, and the way people experience place mean that it becomes an interesting and useful way of allowing us to observe, analyse and understand different worlds. Place is also critical in creating and maintaining identity, both individual and group, and is strongly linked to ideas and feelings of belonging (Price 2013: 158; Taylor 2010: 13). This is emphasised by the importance of place in how we understand the world both today, and how we draw on it in creating understandings about our pasts: "Not only is place central to accounts of how the world as we know it came to be, place is also central to historical accounts of how we came to know our world and our place in it" (Price 2013: 158). Place can also be an analytical tool, a means of seeing, knowing and understanding the world, and work by geographers such as Massey (2002) and Cresswell (2015: 18) shows that societies can be analysed through their attachments, connections and their experience of place. Place also has resonance for archaeologists, as places are one of the primary settings for archaeological explorations; it is where we do things.

Explorations of identity, of who we are, have a very strong link to place, and in particular resonate with the idea of "home" or where people feel "at home" (e.g. Acuff 2012: 136; Antonisch 2010: 646; O"Gorman 2014; Teerling 2011). A summary of this idea argues that "Belonging... is about shared experiences, values, networks and practices, and the ways in which such connections are manifested in everyday life and in emotions of inclusivity" (Teerling 2011: 1083). Contributing to home as a place, structures, possessions, attachments (to people and the physical manifestations), and lived experiences all play a significant role (Acuff 2012: 136; Jones – Krzyzanowski 2008: 41). Of course, like any construct home and belonging can be exclusive and can use difference as a basis for division and exclusion, and it is important to avoid essentialising home (and place and belonging). Being reflexive is necessary here, through recognising that home is more than physical elements of place, and that home and belonging change over time and in different contexts, just as place does (Jones –Kryzanowski 2008).

A significant element of place and belonging are the memories that are linked to a particular place, and this includes memory of the routine and the regular or everyday, as well as the exceptional (Bourdieu 1977; Viscomi 2010: 17). The activities that people carry out in places help to shape the ways in which they view and understand the world, just as these activities also shape the place or space itself. Buildings can symbolise and embody many things for people, and can be powerful repositories of memory (Bevan 2006). Buildings, and of course place more generally, are the settings and backdrops for both memories of everyday life, of significant and regular events and rituals, and of the extraordinary and unexpected events (Cresswell 2015; Halbwachs 1992 (1952)). Belonging to place, to groups, to communities is deeply connected to memory, and has a major role in identity creation and affirmation (Halbwachs 1992 (1952); Hoelscher – Alderman 2004; Truc 2011). Memory is arguably something that we actively create in the present and is subject to continual revision; memory is a vital and integral part of all of us as humans.

Individual and social memories dominated our work in Bat; the individuals that we interviewed offered selections of their own particular memories of place and life, and when people talked to us in small groups they offered different memories of the same events, activities or places. Difference in memory is critical to recognise, and takes on greater significance when places are being treated as heritage, and this is true for mudbrick villages in Oman as much as any other place where communities are involved in multiple ways in heritage work (Young 2019).

In making the link between these concepts of belonging, memory and place and the historical archaeology work at Bat, the project was centred around learning more about the everyday and the lives and memories of "ordinary" people who have lived in the village, alongside their participation in and witness of some of the major changes in Oman in the recent past. Analyses of the material of an "ordinary" village such as Bat is a very under-utilised means of thinking through the lifeways of its inhabitants and their everyday practices, as well as learning more about the impacts of national and international issues and events on lives (and of course the impacts of people on these issues and events). Different memories were gathered through interviews with people who had lived in the mudbrick houses, site visits and discussions around standing or demolished structures and places, and exploration of excavations and the features and artefacts uncovered.

Conclusion

It is clear that it is deeply important to many individuals at Bat – the older people feel very strongly about the mudbrick village and it allows them to remember an earlier time, a different time. They value the mudbrick as a source of memory about family and community, and it clearly gives them a profound sense of belonging and a profound sense of place. One of our interviewees told us that "Mudbrick is the story of the past and living in the past" (Shakya pers. comm. 2015), which is an incredibly powerful statement that draws together the concepts of memory, belonging and place. Taking the approach of an historical archaeology project has allowed us to go beyond interviews of former occupants of the mudbrick and explore the buildings and place itself through buildings analysis, planning, and excavation which has added layers of information and areas for interpretation. It has shown links between the prehistoric past and the historic past, and shown that different aspects of landscape and structures can shape the ways places develop. Our work in Bat has shown that there are physical links to a very deep past going back thousands of years. Whether or not this much older past is explicitly acknowledged or understood as such, it clearly plays a role in the character and form of place here. The artefact analysis has drawn attention to a very clear horizon apparent in the material culture in the second half of the 20th century. Even though we are not yet sure whether this horizon came about due to the compression of the Imamate in the 1950s or the accession of HM Sultan Qaboos in the 1970s and his *nahḍa*, these two events are connected, and have contributed to the major changes recorded throughout Oman, and clearly visible here at Bat in both buildings and artefacts.

Drawing together different types of evidence and approaches to studying the mudbrick village has allowed us to offer different ways of thinking about the value and significance of these older settlements. The move from mudbrick houses to concrete houses is a symbol of the fundamental political and social changes of the later 20th century, and the remaining mudbrick houses and other structures provide a powerful place that represents a particular past, and are holders and hooks for memory of a way of life that has now changed forever. By valuing the quotidian and the vanishing remnants of a past way of life it is also possible to offer up entirely new ways of thinking about what is important to preserve and how to present it (Young 2019). The mudbrick oases of Oman are very special places in many different ways as repositories of memory, identity and family.

References

Acuff, J. M. 2012
Spectacle and space in the creation of premodern and modern polities: Towards a mixed ontology of collective identity, *International Political Sociology* 6, 132–148. DOI:10.1111/j.1749-5687.2012.00155.x

Al Jahwari, N. 2006
Ancient quarters in Oman: An urgency in the archaeology of Oman, in: Ministry of Heritage and Culture – UNESCO World Heritage Centre (eds), *Proceedings of the Regional Seminar on the Conservation of Earthen Structures in the Arab Countries*, Muscat, 35–44.

Allen, C. H. 1987
Oman. The modernization of the Sultanate, Boulder, Colorado.

Antonisch, M. 2010
Searching for belonging – An analytical framework, *Geography Compass* 4/6, 644–659. DOI:10.1111/j.1749-8198.2009.00317.x

Bandyopadhyay, S. 2011
Manah. An Omani oasis, an Arabian legacy. Architecture and social history of an Omani settlement, Liverpool.

Bevan, R. 2006
The destruction of memory: Architecture at war, London.

Biezeveld, I. 2022
Re(dis)covering the recent: Surveying settlements and society in Central Oman from the 17th to the 20th centuries, *Arabian Archaeology and Epigraphy*, 107–121. DOI:10.1111/aae.12225

Bourdieu, P. 1977
Outline of a theory of practice, Cambridge [translated by R. Nice].

Brooks, A. 2014
Al Ain 19th- and 20th-century European-tradition ceramics and glass report: Khrais and Qatara [unpublished report].

Brooks, A. – Young, R. 2016
Historical archaeology and heritage in the Middle East: A preliminary overview, *Historical Archaeology* 50/4, 22–35. DOI:10.1007/BF03379198

Carter, R. A. 2011
Ceramics of the Qatar National Museum A report and catalogue [unpublished report].

Chatty, D. 2013
Rejecting Authenticity in the Desert Landscapes of the Modern Middle East: Development Processes in the Jiddat Il-Harasiis, Oman, in: S. Hafez - S. Slyomovics (eds) *Anthropology of the Middle East and North Africa: Into the New Millennium*, Bloomington, 145–164.

Clark, T. 2008
Oman, in: H. Arbuthnott – R. Muir – T. Clark (eds), *British missions around the Gulf, 1575–2005: Iran, Iraq, Kuwait, Oman*, Folkestone.

Cresswell, T. 2015
Place. An introduction. Chichester, West Sussex [2nd edition].

Graz, L. 1982
The Omanis. Sentinels of the Gulf, London.

Grey, A. 2011
Late trade wares on Arabian shores: 18th- to 20th-century imported fineware ceramics from excavated sites on the southern Persian (Arabian) Gulf coast, *Post-Medieval Archaeology* 45/2, 350–373. DOI:10.1179/174581311X13135030529557

Halbwachs, M. 1992
On Collective Memory, Chicago [edited and translated by L. A. Coster].

Hoelscher, S. – Alderman, D. H. 2004
Memory and place: Geographies of a critical relationship, *Social and Cultural Geography* 5/3, 347–355. DOI:10.1080/1464936042000252769

Jones, P. – Krzyzanowski, M. 2008
Identity, belonging and migration: Beyond constructing 'others', in: G. Delanty – R. Wodak – P. Jones (eds), *Identity, belonging and migration*, Liverpool, 38–53.

Massey, D. 2002
Globalisation: What does it mean for geography? *Geography* 87/4: 293–296.

Massey, D. 1994
Space, place and gender, Cambridge.

O'Gorman, E. 2014
Belonging, *Environmental Humanities* 5: 283–286. DOI:10.1215/22011919-3615523

Owtram, F. 2004
A modern history of Oman. Formation of the state since 1920, London.

Price, P. L. 2013
Place, in: N. C. Johnson – R. H. Schein – J. Winders (eds), *The Wiley-Blackwell companion to cultural geography*, London, 157–170.

Sasaki, H. – Sasaki, T. 2012
Trade ceramics from East Asia to the Arabian Peninsula, in: D. Potts – P. Hellyer (eds), *Fifty years of Emirates archaeology. Proceedings of the second international conference on the archaeology of the United Arab Emirates*, Dubai, 105–120.

Taylor, S. 2010
Narratives of Identity and Place, London.

Teerling, J. 2011
The development of new 'third-cultural spaces of belonging': British-born Cypriot 'return' migrants in Cyprus, *Journal of Ethnic and Migration Studies* 37/7, 1079–1099. DOI: 10.1080/1369183X.2011.572484

Thornton, C. – Cable, C. – Possehl, G. 2016
The Bronze Age towers at Bat, Sultanate of Oman: Research by the Bat Archaeological Project, 2007–12, Pennsylvania.

Truc, G. 2011
Memory of places and places of memory: For a Halbwachsian socio-ethnography of collective memory, *International Social Science Journal* 62/203-204, 147–159. DOI: 10.1111/j.1468-2451.2011.01800.x

UNESCO 2023
Archaeological sites of Bat, Al-Khutm and Al-Ayn, http://whc.unesco.org/en/list/434 [accessed 26.04.2023]

Valeri, M. 2009
Oman. Politics and society in the Qaboos state, New York.

Viscomi, J. 2010
"The farthest place" Social boundaries in an Egyptian desert community, Cairo/New York.

Wellsted, J. R. 1978 (1838)
Travels in Arabia 1, Graz.

Young, R. 2019
Historical archaeology and heritage in the Middle East, London.

Young, R. – Al-Jassassi, A. – Al-Shaqsi, A. – Al-Jabri, S. – Batchelor, O. – Dance, K. – De Leon, N. – Humes, A. – Hunt, H. – Riaz, A. – Taha, S. – Cable, C. – Thornton, C. – Zäuner, S. 2018
Bat Oasis Historical Archaeology Project: Interim report on 2014 field season, *The Journal of Oman Studies* 19, 1–18.

Documentation of Omani Traditional Settlements (*Ḥārāt*)

Reality and Aspirations

Ali bin Hamood Al Mahrooqi

Introduction

The old residential settlements, *ḥārāt*, represent a significant aspect of Oman's urban heritage vocabulary. Despite being abandoned only a few decades ago, they continue to be a prominent feature of the Omani built heritage, evident across diverse regions and landscapes. One of the most significant challenges in preserving these settlements is the impact of environmental factors, including rain and weathering, which have eroded parts of these uninhabited settlements. Furthermore, the impact of human activity, including urban sprawl, migration and the use of modern materials, has also had an effect on the preservation and transformation of these settlements. This article examines the realities and aspirations of the Omani Traditional Settlements Listing Project, which was initiated in 2007 by the Ministry of Heritage and Culture (now Tourism).

Traditional settlements in the context of Oman's archaeological heritage

The strategic location of the Sultanate of Oman in the southeast corner of the Arabian Peninsula has played a significant role in the flourishing of its civilization throughout history. Situated between two distinct regions, the sand desert in the southwest and the coastal line in the northeast, some scholars have described Oman as an island within an island (Cleuziou – Tosi 2018: 6). The Hajar Mountains, reaching up to 3,000 metres in height, form the backbone of the northern part of the Sultanate of Oman. The coastal line of the Indian Ocean extends for over 600 km, from Musandam in the extreme north to Ras al Hadd on the north-eastern tip of the Arabian Peninsula. On the opposite side, the arid region between the mountains and plains across Dhofar Governorate is home to a rich array of natural resources, which have enabled the local inhabitants to settle and thrive since the early Stone Age (Fig. 1).

The Bronze Age, spanning from 5,100 to 3,700 years ago, saw the emergence of significant civilizational developments in society, economy, and architecture, particularly along the fertile

in: S. Döpper – B. Mershen – J. Kanditt – I. Biezeveld – T. Schmidt-Lux (eds) 2025, *Mudbrick Settlements of the Oman Peninsula. Inhabited – Abandoned – Re(dis)covered*, Leiden: Sidestone Press, 51–66.

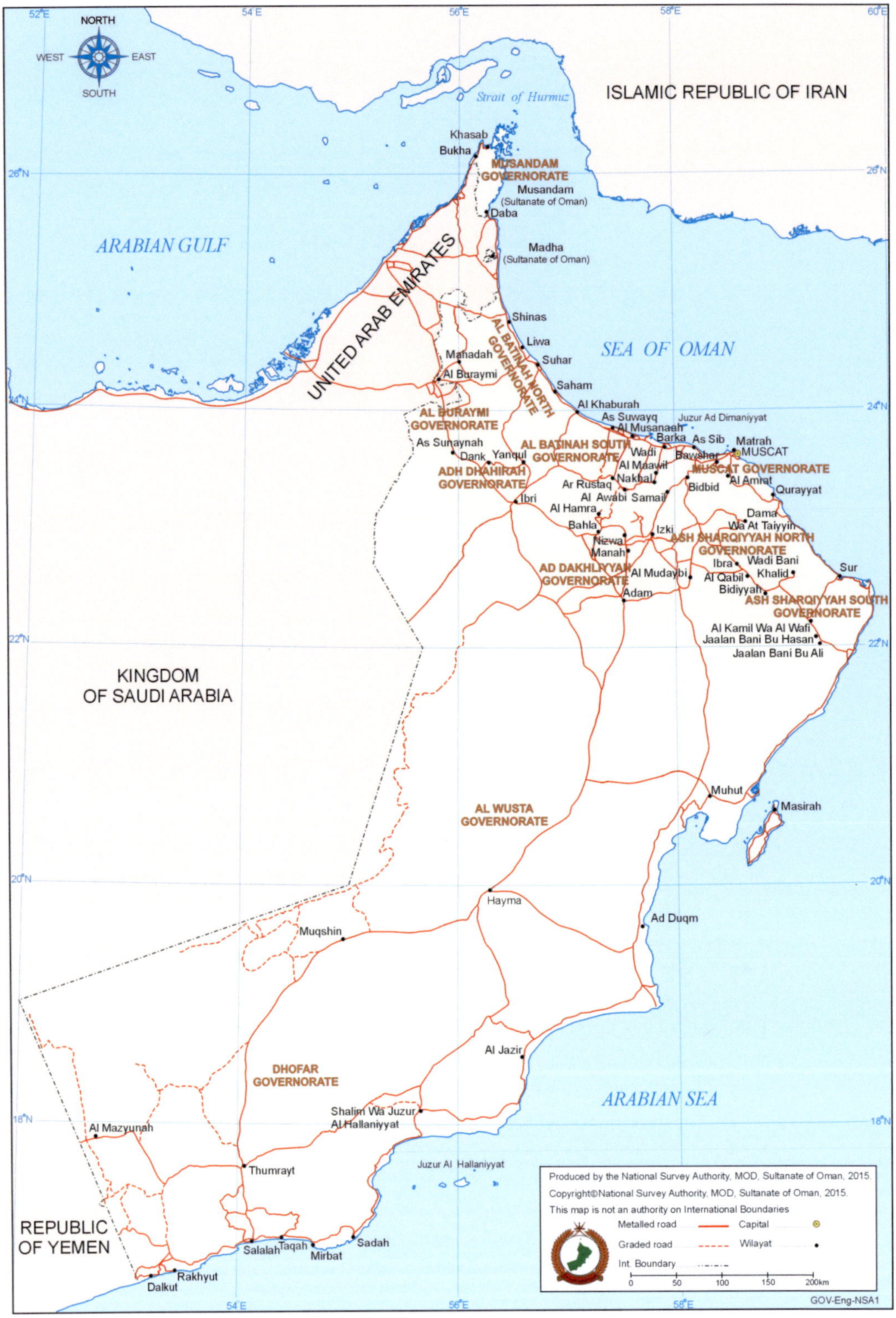

Fig. 1: Map of the Sultanate of Oman.

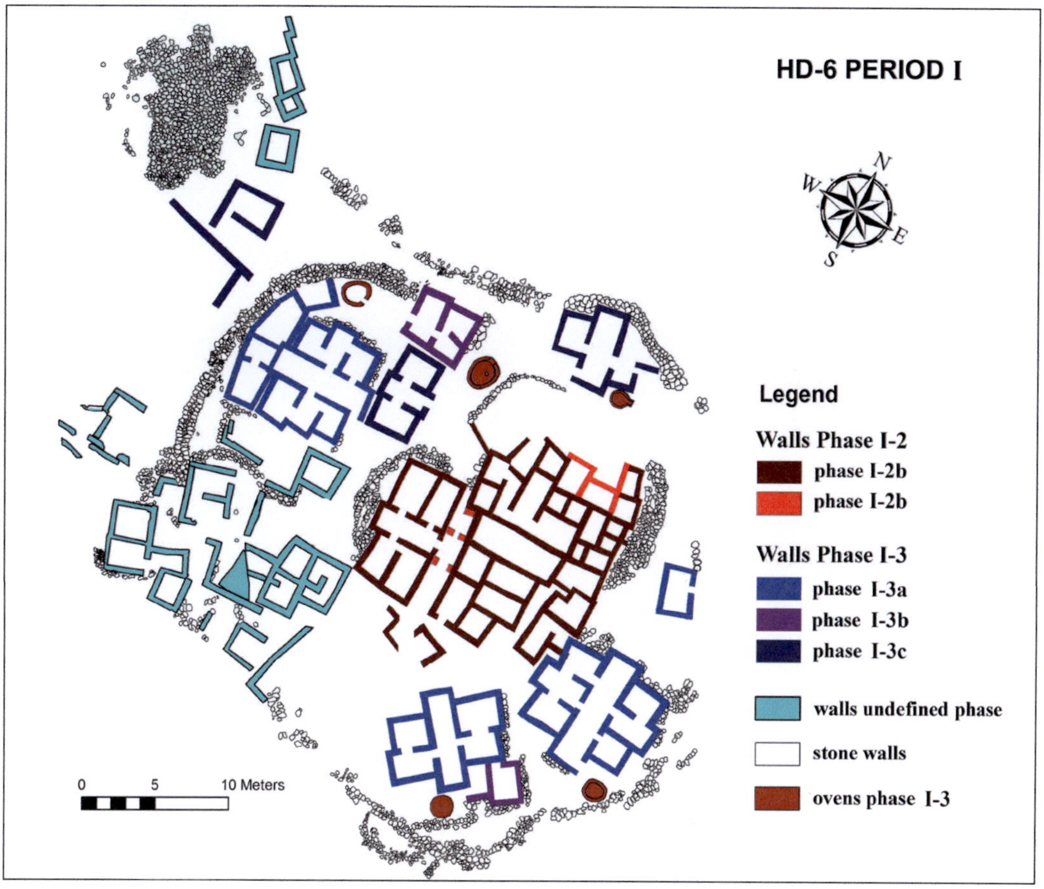

Fig. 2: Plan of the Early Bronze Age settlement Ras al Hadd HD-6 (plan: MHT/Maurizio Cattani).

foothills of the Hajar Mountains. The archaeological discoveries demonstrate a high level of human knowledge, organisation, and trade ties with neighbouring communities, including Mesopotamia, the Indus Valley Civilisation, and the Ancient Egyptian Civilisation. Mineral extraction, in particular of copper, constituted a significant aspect of the economy of that period. Monumental structures of unknown function, referred to as towers, appeared, and burials were practiced in elaborate above-ground stone tombs. The Bronze Age settlements provide evidence of the sophisticated design and planning techniques employed during that period. During this period, the use of traditional mud-based masonry commenced a long-lasting success story in the Sultanate of Oman. Examples of Bronze Age mudbrick architecture can be observed in archaeological sites such as Al Khashbah, Al Gharyein, Ras al Jinz and Ras al Hadd. The archaeological sites provide evidence of well-planned and organised settlements (Cleuziou – Tosi 2018). The settlement of Ras al Hadd, for instance, is characterised by a dense accumulation of several tripartite houses constructed from mudbrick, surrounded by a stone wall (Fig. 2).

During this period and the subsequent one, Omani architecture underwent a process of evolution and differentiation. Three principal types of religious, civil, and defensive architecture emerged over time, each catering to the specific needs of Omani society. Today, the Sultanate of Oman is home to numerous traditional historical settlements, castles, forts,

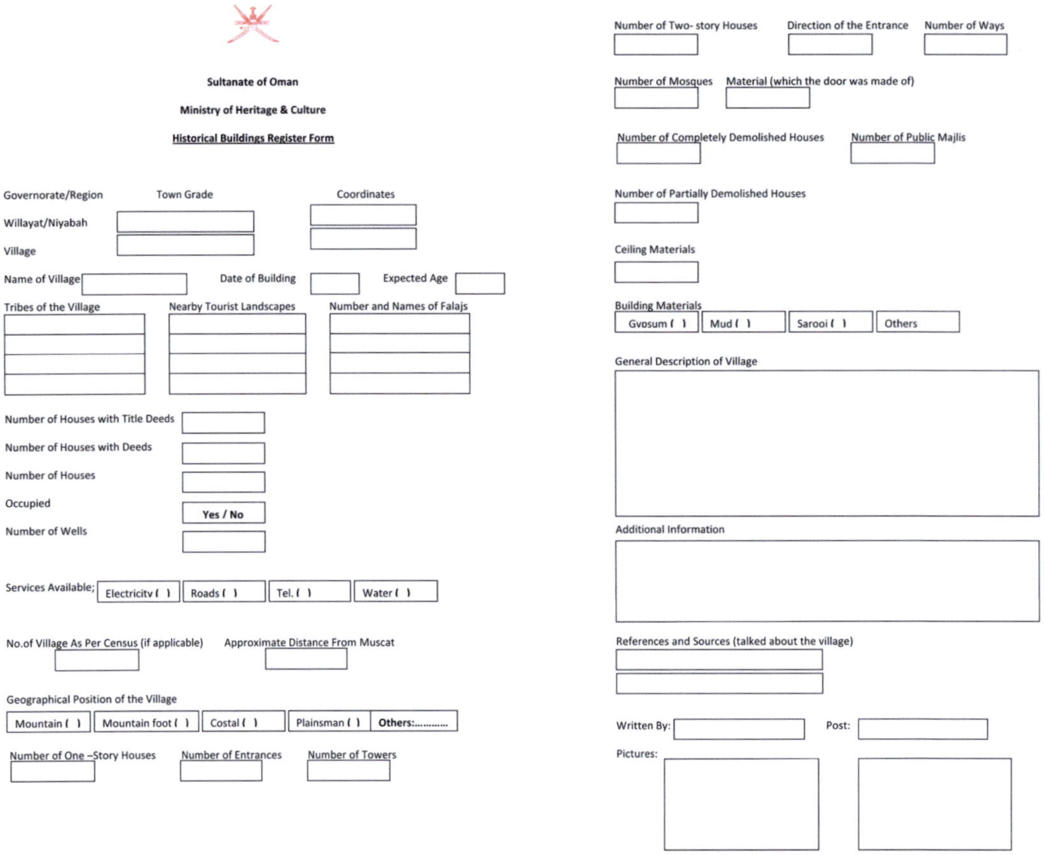

Sultanate of Oman

Ministry of Heritage & Culture

Historical Buildings Register Form

Governorate/Region — Town Grade — Coordinates

Willayat/Niyabah

Village

Name of Village — Date of Building — Expected Age

Tribes of the Village — Nearby Tourist Landscapes — Number and Names of Falajs

Number of Houses with Title Deeds

Number of Houses with Deeds

Number of Houses

Occupied: Yes / No

Number of Wells

Services Available; Electricitv ( ) Roads ( ) Tel. ( ) Water ( )

No.of Village As Per Census (if applicable) — Approximate Distance From Muscat

Geographical Position of the Village: Mountain ( ) Mountain foot ( ) Costal ( ) Plainsman ( ) Others:...........

Number of One –Story Houses — Number of Entrances — Number of Towers

Number of Two- story Houses — Direction of the Entrance — Number of Ways

Number of Mosques — Material (which the door was made of)

Number of Completely Demolished Houses — Number of Public Majlis

Number of Partially Demolished Houses

Ceiling Materials

Building Materials: Gvpsum ( ) Mud ( ) Sarooi ( ) Others

General Description of Village

Additional Information

References and Sources (talked about the village)

Written By: — Post:

Pictures:

Fig. 3: Documentation form used in the Omani Traditional Settlements Listing Project.

and shrines, which showcase the dominant architectural style, which reflects the climatic conditions of the region. Over the course of Oman's history, local architecture has evolved considerably, adapting to the fluctuating natural factors while persistently seeking to develop a settlement pattern that provides sufficient protection and meets the needs of their lifestyle.

Omani Traditional Settlements Listing Project

Traditional settlements (*ḥārāt*) of historical significance represent a fundamental aspect of the old Omani architectural heritage. These settlements are held in high emotional esteem by the Omani people, who regard them as an integral part of the country's visual landscape. Their distinctive topography and rich cultural heritage contribute to the overall character of Oman. At an early stage, the Ministry of Heritage and Tourism initiated a number of programmes and enacted legislation with the objective of safeguarding this cultural heritage. In 2007, the Ministry of Heritage and Culture established a national committee chaired by the Undersecretary for Heritage Affairs, comprising representatives from the Ministry of Tourism, Ministry of the Interior, Ministry of Regional Municipalities and Water Resources, Ministry of Housing, Muscat Municipality and Dhofar Municipality, with the objective of registering and protecting historic buildings. This initiative led to the establishment of the Omani Traditional Settlements Listing Project.

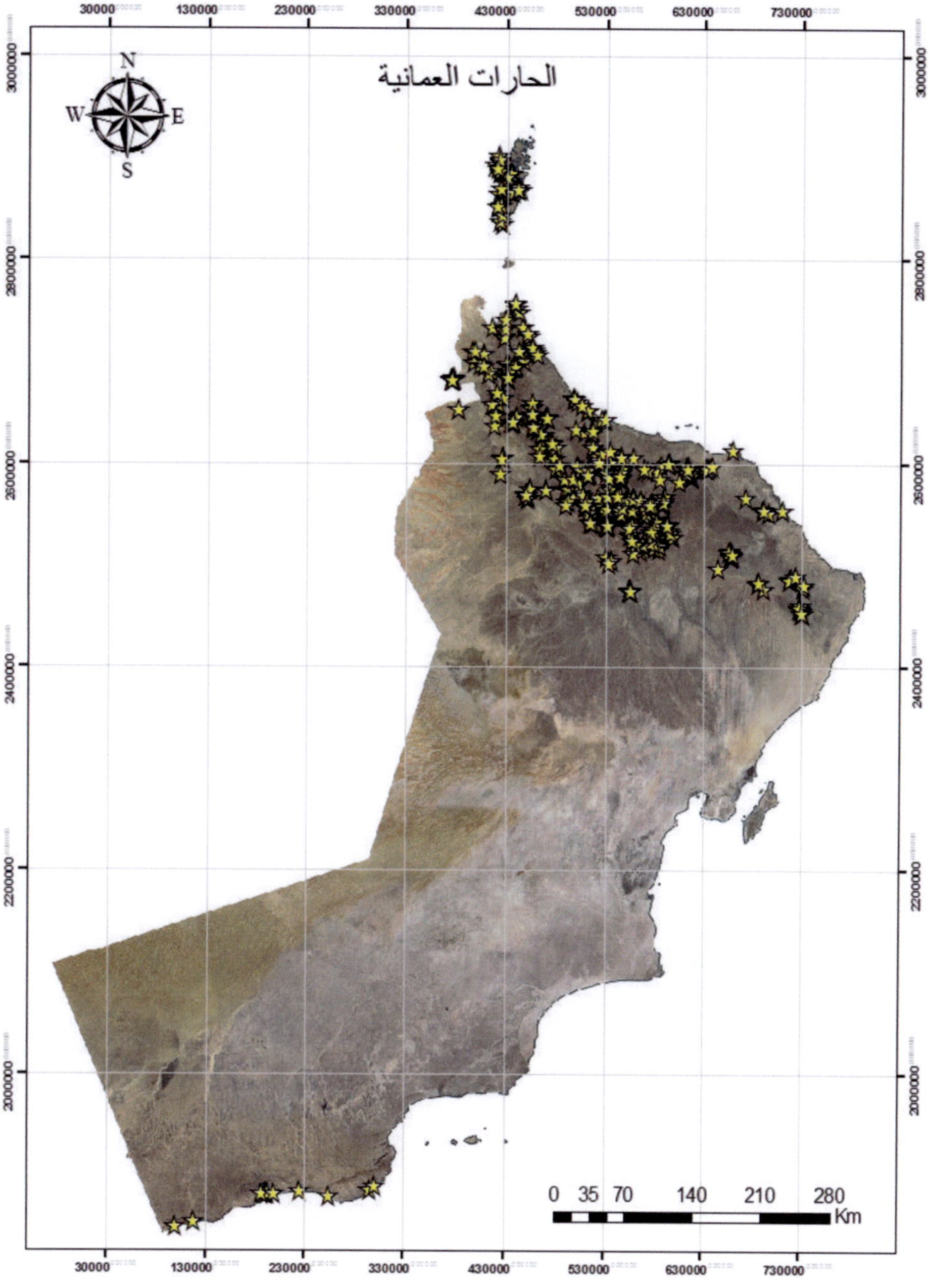

Fig. 4: Yellow stars show distribution of traditional settlements recorded in the Omani Traditional Settlements Listing Project.

The principal objective of the committee was to compile and identify the distribution and size of the settlements as part of the cultural heritage of the Sultanate of Oman. The projects employed a conventional documentation strategy, whereby local communities completed forms with the necessary information (Fig. 3). Subsequently, teams from the Ministry of Heritage and Tourism conducted on-site inventories, which included the documentation of

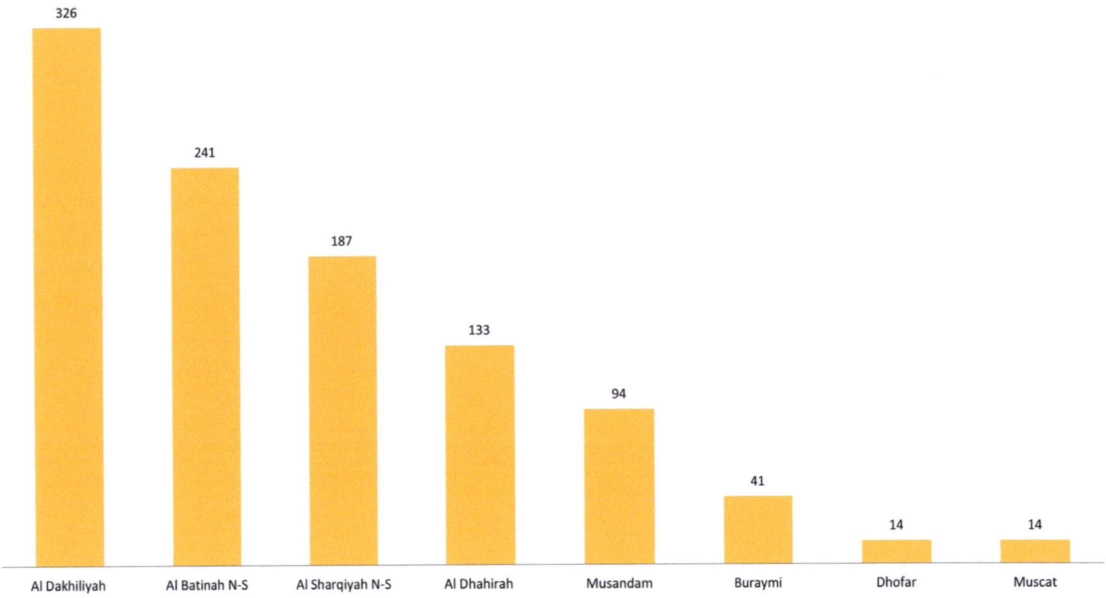

Fig. 5: Distribution of traditional settlements according to governorate.

site descriptions, photography, and ethnographic research on settlement and population, tribal composition, ownership, and other pertinent aspects. This was done in order to obtain the necessary information to create a database for the Omani vernacular settlements. As a result, 1,050 sites have been registered across different governorates (Fig. 4 and Fig. 5) (Al Mahrouqi 2009).

That was followed by awareness campaigns addressing the various segments of Omani society underlining the need to safeguard and preserve the settlements. Further, in meeting no. 2006/149 the cabinet issued Circular No. 535/102, calling for the preservation of the traditional settlements (*ḥārāt*). Upon the completion of the initial phase of the project, which resulted in the creation of a database containing information on the settlements and their geographic distribution within the Sultanate, their structural status, architectural components, and other relevant data, the committee compiled a report detailing the size and distribution of settlements in each governorate. Furthermore, the committee classified the settlements into three categories (1-2-3) according to their structural condition, in addition to several other criteria that were endorsed by the committee to guide future action (Fig. 6). The preservation of these settlements continued to be a priority while pursuing a comprehensive development agenda (Al Mahrouqi 2009: 5).

In the second phase of the project, the committee collaborated with international experts and local and international academic institutions. During this phase, a number of *ḥārāt* were documented, including Harat Al Saybani in Birkat al Mawz (Oman Committee 2014a) and Harat Al Yaman in Izki (Oman Committee 2014b). The projects entailed the production of comprehensive architectural documentation, the identification of potential threats and the development of restoration strategies, as well as the creation of visitor facilities and management plans for the *ḥārāt* selected for future reuse. To date, twelve *ḥārāt* have been fully documented and surveyed architecturally, while architectural surveys have been

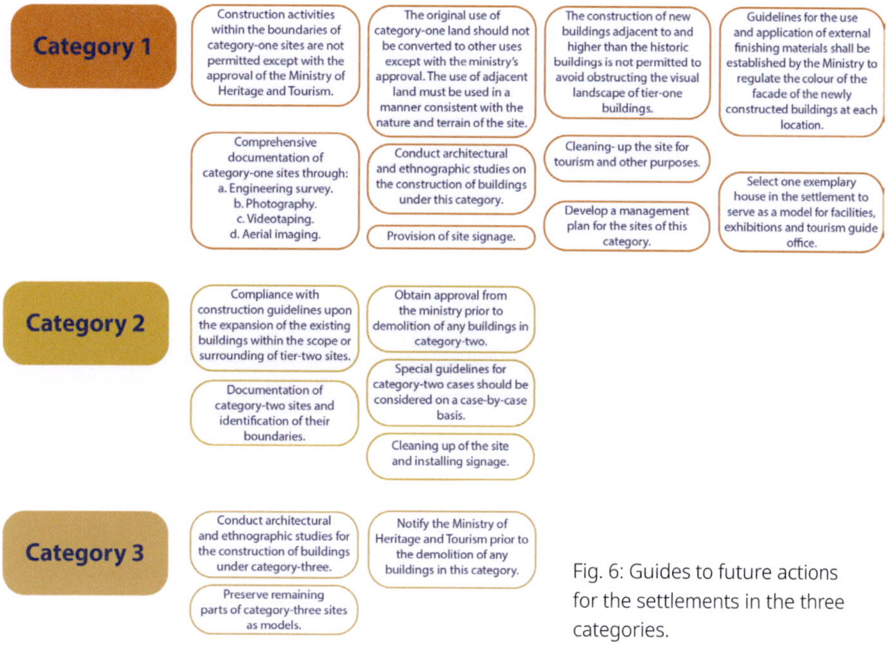
Category 1
Construction activities within the boundaries of category-one sites are not permitted except with the approval of the Ministry of Heritage and Tourism.
The original use of category-one land should not be converted to other uses except with the ministry's approval. The use of adjacent land must be used in a manner consistent with the nature and terrain of the site.
The construction of new buildings adjacent to and higher than the historic buildings is not permitted to avoid obstructing the visual landscape of tier-one buildings.
Guidelines for the use and application of external finishing materials shall be established by the Ministry to regulate the colour of the facade of the newly constructed buildings at each location.
Comprehensive documentation of category-one sites through: a. Engineering survey. b. Photography. c. Videotaping. d. Aerial imaging.
Conduct architectural and ethnographic studies on the construction of buildings under this category.
Provision of site signage.
Cleaning- up the site for tourism and other purposes.
Develop a management plan for the sites of this category.
Select one exemplary house in the settlement to serve as a model for facilities, exhibitions and tourism guide office.
Category 2
Compliance with construction guidelines upon the expansion of the existing buildings within the scope or surrounding of tier-two sites.
Obtain approval from the ministry prior to demolition of any buildings in category-two.
Documentation of category-two sites and identification of their boundaries.
Special guidelines for category-two cases should be considered on a case-by-case basis.
Cleaning up of the site and installing signage.
Category 3
Conduct architectural and ethnographic studies for the construction of buildings under category-three.
Notify the Ministry of Heritage and Tourism prior to the demolition of any buildings in this category.
Preserve remaining parts of category-three sites as models.

Fig. 6: Guides to future actions for the settlements in the three categories.

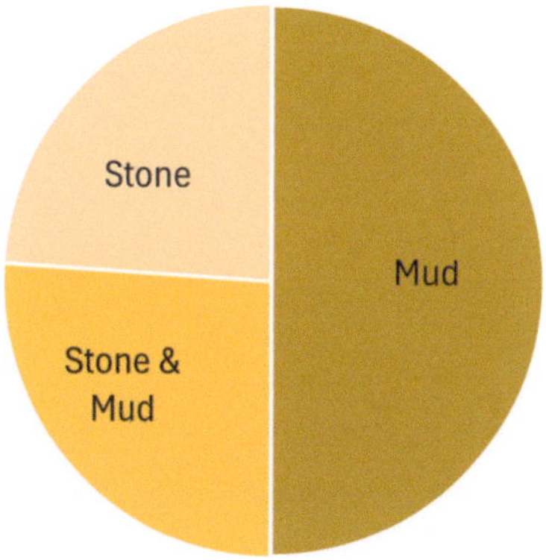
Stone
Mud
Stone & Mud

Fig. 7: Building material used for in the different registered *ḥārāt*.

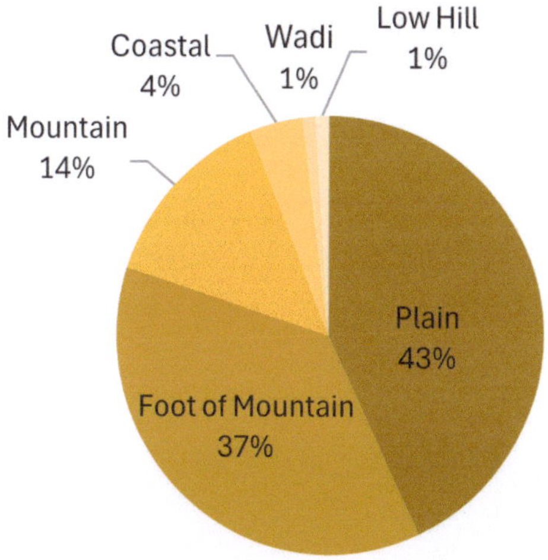
Coastal 4%
Wadi 1%
Low Hill 1%
Mountain 14%
Plain 43%
Foot of Mountain 37%

Fig. 8: Distribution of *ḥārāt* according to their geographic location.

conducted for a further twenty *ḥārāt*. The Ministry intends to continue the documentation programme, with the objective of successively encompassing all registered *ḥārāt*.

A variety of analyses can be conducted on the registered settlements using the information in the database generated by the Omani Traditional Settlements Listing Project. With regard to the building materials, it can be observed that 50% of the settlements in the Sultanate of Oman were constructed using mudbricks, while the remaining 50% were predominantly built using a combination of stone and mud (Fig. 7). As mentioned earlier, the genuine architectural heritage is influenced by local values and environmental factors. Since the natural environment in Oman is remarkably diverse, the same applies to the building materials too. The availability of building materials across different regions of the Sultanate of Oman largely determines this distribution.

Furthermore, the data provide insight into the geographic distribution of vernacular/traditional settlements. Of these settlements, 43% are located on flat terrain, 37% on foothills, and the remaining 20% are situated along the coastal line, in valleys, and on rocky ridges (Fig. 8).

Characteristics of Omani vernacular settlements

Omani vernacular settlements share a number of spatial, functional and architectural elements. They are typically characterised by densely built-up residential units, with narrow shaded alleys. Functionally, they include both private dwellings and communal spaces, such as mosques and *sablas* (meeting halls), mills and ovens. At the same time, the geographic location and terrain of settlements are concomitant with specific characteristics. Settlements in plains, foothills and valleys typically exhibit multiple defensive structures, such as fortified entrances, walls and towers. In contrast, mountain settlements are generally devoid of towers and fortified entrances. Furthermore, there are usually no congregational mosques in mountain settlements. Similarly, settlements in the mountains generally lack other public structures, such as markets and service centres, due to spatial constraints and their comparatively small size. Multi-storey structures and vertical expansions are more characteristic of settlements situated on flat terrain.

With regard to the planning of settlements, it is evident that free-standing structures are often found in smaller mountain settlements, such as those in the mountains of Musandam or the shepherds' settlements in the western Hajar Mountains. In contrast, attached building structures are common in settlements built in the plains. The town planning principles in the *ḥārāt* reflect those of Islamic town planning, including the safeguarding of privacy and the maintenance of good neighbourly relations. In contrast, it is evident that the planning and construction of villages did not occur in a single, unified manner, but rather over an extended period of time. This process was influenced by a number of factors, including Islamic traditions and norms, architectural planning, and various environmental considerations (Okasha 1994: 61).

In the following section, an overview of the most distinctive features of Omani *ḥārāt* will be provided.

(1) Dwellings

Shelter is a basic human need, and it is necessary to everyone. Ensuring adequate housing has always been a concern depending on the economic circumstances and the availability of building materials. Houses are important because the architectural elements of dwellings are a tangible representation of deep-seated Islamic beliefs, values and the life of the communities within them including the environment. The house plan and size vary depending on the number of family members, income and social status (Mershen 1998: 206).

The ground floor in Omani houses is used as a store for food and dates, as well as an enclosure for animals, a water well, a women's prayer hall and the corridor, which is considered as a connection and movement element to access the entire house facilities. Further, it serves as a ventilator for the facilities of the ground floor, which contains several rooms, used as accommodation or guest rooms. The upper floor is usually used as a living space that contains the bedroom and living room and a kitchen. In some larger houses, there is an opening on the top floor through which water is channelled from the ground floor to other floors such as in castles and forts (Uthman 1999: 188).

The houses are constructed side by side with no gaps, and the rooftops are no different; a low rise partition wall is erected to define roof boundaries but allows residents of the adjacent houses to exchange food and other items. Most houses in old Omani neighbourhoods (*ḥārāt*) are built from mudbricks and consist of two floors, but foundations are usually constructed using stone blocks.

The Architectural Elements in Old Dwellings

Doors: The old Omani neighbourhoods still maintain decorated wooden doors with hard-carved inscriptions. The main gate is usually a double-winged door to enable the entry of tools and supplies. However, the doors of rooms and other utilities are smaller double-winged or single-winged doors. The parts of the door are fixed using the strongest type of nails. A pointed arch is constructed on top of the door.

Arches: Arches have many different shapes depending on the arrangements of the building. The pointed arches carry the load of the roofs of shops in the alleys in the neighbourhood (*ḥārāt*). Other shapes of arches include the triangular and ogee arch in the halls, openings on top of the entrances, the gun holes in towers, in addition to the facades of the houses and shelves on the walls.

Staircases: A staircase is an important component of a building providing access to different floors and roofs of the building. Some houses have two staircases. The turnaround staircases are usually constructed to the right side of the main entrance to reduce the steepness of the stairs and facilitate their use by elderly people.

Shelves: The rooms in old houses have multiple shelves *(rawzana)* and openings with pointed or triangular shapes as high as one and a half meters. They are divided into two sections – the upper section is used to store valuable and fragile items and the lower section is used to store heavy and less important items. The shelves are divided by using flat wood.

Decorative elements: Stucco works were noticed in numerous houses, mosques and public spaces. The ornaments of the doors and windows vary greatly with mosaic patterns ranging between geometrical and botanical with no human or animal images because they are not allowed according to Islamic teachings. Most of the roofs are painted white and red. The writings on the roofs and walls of the living room on the upper floor may show the date of construction in the Hijri calendar. Sometimes they may contain poetry or traditional Sunnah lines of teaching, floral ornaments – palms fronds – or perhaps geometric elements like circles, rhombuses or ripple zigzags.

(2) Mosques

The significance of mosques in Islamic architecture is evident in their role as centres for Islamic faith, principles, and values, which are shaped by environmental factors, local customs, and traditions. Historic mosques in the interior regions of Oman were typically built without minarets, while the *miḥrāb* (niche) remained a simple concave in the *qibla* wall for centuries. The Sultanate of Oman is home to thousands of mosques and places of worship that continue to foster the principles that have been glorified by mosques since the inception of Islam (Costa 2006: 78).

The geographic location of Oman has led to the development of two distinct types of mosques. The first are those found in the interior region, which are typically constructed as simple structures similar to residential houses and lack minarets, a feature that is common for mosques in other Islamic countries. The second are those found in the coastal areas, which have been influenced by external factors due to trade exchange and maritime interactions with other nations and civilisations (Jeroffs 2012: 24). Mosques along the Batinah coast and in Muscat often display Indo-Persian decorative influences and symbols while Yemeni artistic influences can be discovered in mosques in Dhofar Governorate.

The strong local values and climatic factors inspired the architectural fabric of the mosques in Oman. They have gained a real sense of uniqueness as they are passionately associated with the values of the Ibadi sect of Islam. Ibadi mosques are characterised by their plain exterior facades, with the main element of decoration focused upon the *miḥrāb*. Moreover, the geographic location and natural elements meant that they were less affected by cultural influences from outside, thus preserving their genuine architectural style and distinctive identity until very recently. Generally, mosques are classified into six groups according to their use (Jeroffs 2012: 80–82): Jamiʿ Mosques (where Jumʿah prayers take place such as at Nizwa Mosque), Fardh Mosques (where the five daily prayers take place), ʿUbbad Mosques (this type of mosque is usually constructed in the wilderness, cemeteries, and mountains away from houses), Al Mazaarah Mosques (this type is usually constructed between greenery, Eid prayer areas, and cemetery prayer areas). Mosques in Oman vary as per their usage and location, their size and architectural detailing. However, there are common elements shared by most mosques:

Miḥrāb (niche): Ancient mosques were constructed with a simple *miḥrāb* (niche) facing the *qibla*. Over time, this evolved into a frame or set of frames with a pointed or triangular arch on the top. Prior to the seventh Hijri century/13th century CE, the *miḥrāb* was merely a simple niche carved in the *qibla* wall, embellished with intricate ornaments including geometric decorations such as zigzag lines, the sun, the moon, and crescent motifs, rather than floral patterns. The beginning of the seventh century/13th century CE saw a significant shift in construction trends, moving away from deep trenching and multiple overlapping niches towards circular gypsum casts, where a plasterboard decorated with geometric, botanical, and inscribed motifs surrounds the *miḥrāb* niche (Fig. 9). Renowned families, including the Al Hamimi family and the Mashmal carvers, perfected this craft and established an artistic school that left a tangible impact across numerous cities in Oman. The industry of plaster cast *miḥrābs* reached its zenith during the tenth Hijri century/17th century CE (Baldissera 2009: 17).

Prayer hall: Most mosque models are rectangular in shape, featuring rows of columns with variously shaped arches to support the roofs. This architectural feature is a common occurrence in almost all mosques in the Sultanate of Oman.

Fig. 9: A *miḥrāb* in Adam.

Būmah: In place of the conventional tower-shaped minaret, a small dome (*būmah*) has been constructed to cover the exit to the rooftop. This architectural feature serves to prevent the entry of rainwater and dust into the prayer hall.

Ablution area: In many mosques, small rectangular rooms are constructed on top of *falaj* channels for the purpose of washing and ablution. In certain instances, the mosque incorporates an ablution area comprising a well and a water basin, which are flanked by small reservoirs used for washing and ablution. The ablution area must be entirely distinct from the prayer hall, in order to ensure the convenience of the worshippers. In the majority of cases, the ablution area is constructed on the eastern side of the mosque complex, in a location that is separate from the entrance of the prayer hall.

Sabīl: Sabīl is a dedicated shaded area for the drinking of cold water dispensed to passersby. It is a simple structure comprising a metal rack or rope suspended from a tree or ceiling at one end, with water pots (to keep the water cool) at the other end and a reservoir placed underneath to collect water drops falling from the pots.

Ceilings: The ceilings of Al Jamiʿ mosques and Fardh mosques are of considerable height to provide sufficient lighting and ventilation to the prayer hall. They typically reach a height of six metres. Notable examples are the Al Mazaraa, the Al Shawadhina and the Al Shajbi mosques in Nizwa. In contrast, smaller mosques, such as ʿUbbad, Mazaariʿ and cemetery mosques, have relatively low ceilings, not exceeding three metres in height. These ceilings are supported by circular trusses or rectangular beams, which end with pointed or semi-circular arches.

Courtyard: The courtyard of the mosque is a large, open space that is surrounded by a low wall and connects the other units of the mosque complex. The moderate evening climate renders the space conducive to the performance of prayers, which is a more tranquil experience than that afforded by the prayer hall. It is a sacred monument that occupies a special place in the hearts of Muslims, similar to the mosque. In some courtyards, there are multiple entrances and exits that link it to the adjoining units. In other instances, the courtyard is equipped with a single entrance, as is the case with the Al Rahba Mosques and the ʿUbbad mosques.

Fig. 10: A Quran school in Adam.

(3) Quranic and literary schools

Islam places great importance on education, as evidenced by the Prophet's (PBUH) first revelation: "Recite in the name of your Lord who created. Created man from a clinging substance. Recite, and your Lord is the most Generous Who taught by the pen. Taught man that which he knew not" (Surat al Alaq 1-5). Allah says: "Are those who know equal to those who know not?" (Surat al Zumr 9). Moreover, the Prophet (PBUH) encouraged the pursuit of knowledge, stating: "Whoever takes a path upon which to obtain knowledge, Allah makes the path to Paradise easy for him" (Hadith 2646) (Al Khan *et al.* 2001: 191). His successor Caliphs followed his example, using their private residences, mosques, and marketplaces as venues for teaching the Holy Quran.

In addition to the mosques, independent facilities were established for the education of the Quran and literature. As in other Muslim countries, Quranic schools proliferated in Omani villages, where boys and girls were instructed in the Holy Quran, the fundamentals of the Arabic language and numeracy (Fig. 10). Philanthropists were prompt in providing donations and allocating shares of *aflāj* water for fundraising, with the objective of supporting teachers and students and maintaining schools. Even the shadows cast by trees were utilised as makeshift educational facilities.

(4) Cemeteries and shrines

The patterns observed in cemeteries varied over time and place. The shape and size of a cemetery are determined by a number of factors, including religious beliefs, customs and traditions, and economic and social standards. Cemeteries are regarded as a significant repository of Oman's historical record, offering insights into the social, cultural, and religious practices of the past. These insights can be gained from various sources, including memorials, funeral furnishings, and tombstones. They serve as a tangible reminder of bygone economic, social, and religious legacies (Al Mahrouqi 2012: 106). Cemeteries in traditional settlements exhibit a high degree of similarity. Endowments were provided to establish a specific graveyard for a particular group of people, as is the case of the Al Khousa cemetery, Al Aqr

Fig. 11: A general view of the Imams Cemetery in Nizwa, showing gravestones and the ruins of a mausoleum.

village, which was dedicated to the burial of children only. In other locations, a cemetery was established for the interment of individuals who had succumbed to smallpox.

(4) Defensive structures

Defensive structures included settlements that were fortified with towers, walls, and in addition, forts and castles. Such structures constituted a crucial element in the traditional settlements of Oman, while elevated terrain was employed for the construction of watchtowers, which served the dual purpose of surveillance and guarding. This was particularly evident in settlements constructed on hilltops and mountain slopes, such as the Al Saybani settlement at Birkat Al Mawz (Fig. 12). Defensive structures assumed a significant role in shaping history and thought. More than 550 castles and forts, in addition to 1,294 towers and 59 walls, were registered in the Sultanate of Oman.

Entrances: The room accessed from the neighbourhood's gate (*bawāba* or *dirwāza*) is locally called *ṣabāḥ*. This is a transitory space granting access to the *ḥāra* and links it to the outside world. The gate room is usually equipped with two platforms facing one another, where the men of the quarter often sit during their siesta or to chat and make some handicrafts such as palm leaf products and other things. The accesses are usually manned to defend and guard the village against any potential attacks during wars (Office of the Deputy Prime Minister for Cabinet Affairs 2008: 148).

Castles and forts represent one of the most prominent historical and cultural monuments in the Sultanate of Oman. They are regarded as a repository of cultural heritage, providing insights into pivotal eras in Oman's history and assuming a significant historical significance. In addition to their military function, these structures were also used as governance centres, with some even complemented with schools for education and

Fig. 12: Harat Al Saybani in Birkat Al Mawz (Oman Committee 2014c).

learning. The rule of the Ya'ariba dynasty marked the apogee of the development of local, and especially defensive, architecture. This latter development reflected the emergence of powerful artillery, which necessitated a rethinking of the forts' architectural design and their towers. In contrast to the typical arrangement of multiple smaller towers along the forts' perimeters, a distinctive new design was developed, comprising two massive round cannon towers built diagonally to one another.

Challenges to the preservation of the traditional architecture of Oman

The traditional architecture of Oman is facing a number of significant challenges, both natural and human-made. These include the threat to the structural stability of these monuments posed by factors such as rainwater and weathering, as well as the absence of regular maintenance and restoration, rising temperatures, frigidity, wind humidity, and biodeterioration (insects, grazing animals). However, the rapid urbanisation of the Sultanate of Oman, which commenced in the late 1970s, is regarded as one of the most significant human-induced threats to the safety of local architecture in general and that of settlements in particular. The mass movement of the population has accelerated the decay and loss of historic buildings due to a lack of restoration and renovation. Non-local forms of architecture began to encroach upon the built environment (Taylor-Soubeyran – Vignes-Dumas 1989: 118). Furthermore, the paucity of studies on the extensive Omani architectural heritage has created a significant gap and challenge. The challenges encountered by those in charge of the management of the Sultanate's architectural heritage can only be met by the implementation of management plans that devise options for its sustainable utilisation. This necessitates the garnering of support from the local community to preserve and protect the local heritage through the provision of financial and technical support, the conducting of consultative studies and the implementation of a system of close monitoring of any restoration and renovation activities to prevent further damage to the historic monuments. Consequently, the Omani Traditional Settlements Listing Project has formulated the following recommendations in order to ensure the future of Oman's *ḥārāt*:

- Complete the documentation of local Omani architecture.
- Develop management plans to ensure protection of local architectural heritage.
- Support the efforts of the local community towards the protection and recruitment of the local community.
- Provide restoration materials and technical support to protect architectural heritage.
- Engage the local community in the management of local heritage.
- Develop a settlement risk management plan.

References

Al Khan, M. S. – Bagha, M. – Al Sharbaji, A. – Al-Nawawi, M. – Lutfi, M. 2001
Nuzhat al-mutaqīn. Sharḥ Riyādh al-ṣāliḥīn min kalām sayyid al-mursalīn, Beirut.

Al Mahrouqi, A. b. H. 2009
Mashrūʿ ḥaṣr al-ḥārāt al-ʿumānīyya (Omani Traditional Settlements Listing Project (*ḥārāt*)), Muscat. [Report Ministry of Heritage and Culture]

Al Mahrouqi, A. b. H. 2012
Al-majālis al-ʾatharīyya li-wilāyat Adam ʿabr al-tarīkh, in: Literary Forum and Ministry of Heritage and Culture (eds), *Adam ʿabr al-tarīkh*, Muscat, 51–113.

Baldissera, E. 2009
Al-kitābāt fī al-masājid al-ʿumānīyya al-qadīma (Inscriptions in old Omani mosques), Muscat.

Cleuziou, S. – Tosi, M. 2018
In the shadow of the ancestors. The prehistoric foundations of the early arabian civilization in Oman, Muscat.

Costa, P. 2006
Masājid -ʿUmān wa ʾaḍriḥatuha al-tārikhīyya (Historic Mosques and Shrines of Oman), Muscat.

Jeroffs, P. 2012
Amākin al-ṣalāt (Prayer areas), *Al Majd* 20, 20–24.

Mershen, B. 1998
Settlement space and architecture in South Arabian oases – Ethnoarchaeological investigations in recently abandoned settlement quarters in inner Oman, *Proceedings of the Seminar for Arabian Studies* 28, 201–213.

Okasha, T. 1994
Al-qiyyam al-jamālīyya fī al-ʿamāra al-islamīyya (Aesthetic values in Islamic architecture), Cairo.

Office of the Deputy Prime Minister for Cabinet Affairs 2008
The Castles and forts in the Sultanate of Oman, Muscat.

Oman Committee for the Registration and Protection of Historic Building Clusters 2014a
Documentation and Heritage Management Plan for Birkat Al-Mawz: Harat As-Saybani, Muscat.

Oman Committee for the Registration and Protection of Historic Building Clusters 2014b
Documentation and heritage management plan for Izki: Harat Al-Yemen, Muscat.

Oman Committee for the Registration and Protection of Historic Building Clusters 2014c
Harat as-Saybani, Birkat al-Mawz Oasis World Heritage Site (Aflaj Irrigation System), Dakhiliyah Governorate, Muscat.

Taylor-Soubeyran, M. – Vignes-Dumas, C. 1989
Funūn al-ʻamāra al-maḥalīyya fī Salṭanat ʻUmān. [Report UNESCO].

Uthman, M. A. 1999
ʻAmārat al-sudūs al-taqlīdīyya. Dirāsa atharīyya maʻmarīyya. Dirāsat ḥāla, Alexandria.

Reclaimed, Rediscovered or Reinvented

The Changing Perceptions of *Ḥārāt* since the Omani *Nahḍa*

Birgit Mershen

Introduction

Coming to Oman in 1995 to teach at the archaeology department of Sultan Qaboos University, I felt instantly captivated by the Sultanate's built heritage, the beautiful forts and castles, and above all by the innumerable walled mudbrick or stone settlements of central Oman. The oasis towns' residential quarters, *ḥāra*, pl. *ḥārāt*, were generally abandoned or in the process of being abandoned, yet full of relics of past life, constituting archives full of information about the former residents' daily life, social structure, culture and politics (Mershen 1998). My students' reactions to this new Omani field of research were ambivalent. All born several years after Sultan Qaboos acceded to the throne, they conceived of the *ḥārāt* as witnesses of a way of life that was largely beyond their own experience, yet somewhat familiar through the accounts of their parents. While agreeing to acknowledge the abandoned quarters' value as historical and archaeological evidence they saw no need to preserve them, hastening to express satisfaction with their modern accommodation facilities and relief about not having to live in such traditional quarters. Almost three decades later we witness young Omani citizens enjoying an evening around stylish fire bowls at the coffee shop in a restored building in the Harat Al Saybani quarter in Birkat Al Mawz or working as barista at the same venue (Fig. 1 and Fig. 2). Young people engage in workshops at the Sheikh Mohsin Library in the famous sheikh and scholar's repurposed old house in Al Hamra. Omani families take up lodging at heritage accommodations with contemporary en-suite bathrooms in the historic Al 'Aqr quarter next to Nizwa's fort and souq. The sentry walk of the recently refurbished parts of the quarter's historic town wall, which thanks to the addition of ramps and comfortable stairs is accessible to all, in the evenings fills with strolling residents and visitors enjoying the views from above. Furthermore, there are the clean-up campaigns by local sports clubs and citizen initiatives such as in Adam or Al Ghafat, the restoration of an old meeting hall, *sabla*, in Harat Bani Subh, the conversion of families' former homes into private museums, such as in Al Hamra, Misfat Al Abriyin, or

in: S. Döpper – B. Mershen – J. Kanditt – I. Biezeveld – T. Schmidt-Lux (eds) 2025, *Mudbrick Settlements of the Oman Peninsula. Inhabited – Abandoned – Re(dis)covered*, Leiden: Sidestone Press, 67–90.

Fig. 1: Restored gatehouse, Bait Al Sabah, with coffee shop and guest rooms in Harat Al Saybani, Birkat Al Mawz.

Al Rustaq's Al Qasra quarter. Many ancient *ḥārāt* thus appear to have come into the focus of the young generation, sometimes even growing into trendy destinations.

This chapter wants to examine the changing meaning associated with the old residential settlement quarter, *ḥārāt*, since the Omani *nahḍa*. Seeking answers to the question of whether currently expanding private and municipal initiatives may be understood as a kind of reconquest, in the sense that former residents and their descendants are making the *ḥāra* their own again, feeling a renewed emotional connection to it as well as comprehending

Fig. 2: Young Omani barista working at the coffee shop in the restored gatehouse in Harat Al Saybani.

the *ḥāra* as strengthening their cultural identity in a globalized world. Or should current processes be rather understood as a rediscovery or even reinvention of the *ḥāra* under different conditions/terms such as under the aspect of the quarter as an economic asset or an emotive resource?

To examine the changing perceptions of the *ḥārāt*, since the beginning of the Omani *nahḍa* initiated by Sultan Qaboos bin Said upon his accession to rulership in 1970, the present chapter starts with elaborating on the chief elements defining *ḥārāt* as residential quarters. This will be followed by a discussion of the sociocultural effects associated with the move out of traditional neighbourhoods and the move to newly developed residential areas in the last quarter of the 20th century. Perusing the diverse official, scholarly and civil *ḥārāt* discourse and practices during the first two decades of the 21st century and in the age of the renewed "Renaissance" proclaimed by Sultan Haitham bin Tarik succeeding the late Sultan Qaboos in January 2020, the dynamics of a shifting discourse, practices and the different actors associated with current trends in the *ḥārāt* restoration and reuse will be explored.

Ḥārāt – historic residential quarters of Omani oasis towns

Omani oasis towns' historic urban fabric is characterised by its being structured into multiple distinct settlement quarters drawing their water supplies from *aflāj* and wells. The 10th century CE geographer Al Maqdisi (1906: 93) describes Nizwa as a large city with houses built of mud, a Friday mosque located in the wadi and in the heart of the souq, and numerous streams (the *aflāj* channels) and wells from which the residents drew their water. This description of Nizwa as a large oasis town with a total of 89 *aflāj* still applies today. The town's composition of individual quarters is addressed explicitly in Ya'qut Al Hamawi's (died 1228 CE) geographic encyclopedia *Mu'jam al-Buldān* (Al Hamawi 1977: 281). He describes early 13th-century Nizwa as a group of large settlement quarters that are summarised under the name Nizwa. This predominantly tribally defined *ḥāra* structure of oasis towns survives to this day, as do many of the actual historic *ḥārāt*. To this day Nizwa's famous Al Shawadhina Mosque, which was built in the year 7 of Hiijra, 628 CE, is firmly embedded in the urban fabric of the walled Al 'Aqr district, adjoining Nizwa Fort to cite but one example.

Till today larger Omani oasis towns comprise several, sometimes dozens, nowadays mostly abandoned, *ḥārāt*. These compactly built, fortified walled quarters were spread around central urban functions, such as forts, markets and Friday Mosques. While an oasis

Fig. 3: The old *sabla* meeting hall on the first floor of a building in Misfat Al Abriyin.

may comprise multiple historically antagonistic tribes, its *ḥārāt* are inhabited by one or several allied tribal groupings. The individual *ḥāra* represented an independent urban entity that acted as a defensive unit during the raids and tribal feuds still frequent into the second half of the 20th century.

Ḥārāt were often spatially segregated from one another by open areas, gardens, fields or wadis. Located outside of the walled quarters were permanent markets as well as space for seasonal markets, fumes-, bad odour- and noise-producing industries such as blacksmithing, charcoal making, potteries and tanners. At the same time, silversmiths or weavers often had their workshops inside the quarters. A range of communal facilities were integral to a *ḥāra*. It had one or more mosques, male congregational halls, *sabla*, plural *sbal* or *sablāt* (Fig. 3), Quran schools, washing and separate male and female bathing facilities atop the *falaj* channel, *falaj* access points for doing dishes and laundry, and for drawing water for the animals. It included communally used oven pits for the preparation of the festive roast, manually operated grain mills, mortars and other facilities. Of overarching importance for the community's cohesion was the *falaj* water irrigation and distribution system.

From collections of legal cases compiled by Omani legal scholars, such as Abu Said Muhammad bin Said Al Kuddami (305/918–361/972), for example regarding shared house walls and similar items (Al Kuddami 1975: 120–124), we may infer that the 10th century CE *ḥārāt* and their communities did not fundamentally differ from those preserved today. This can be gained, for instance, from discussions and information on building regulations relating to the handling of *falaj* canals leading through residential areas and the construction of bridges or houses over channels, or in building codes that require the front doors and windows of houses facing one another to be positioned offset to prevent the disturbance of residents' privacy by visual corridors. Such rules maintaining good social relations among neighbours equally applied in 20th-century *ḥārāt*. The use of a *ḥāra* was in principle reserved for its residents, who were in close contact with one another. A productive and conflict-free community life in the densely knit quarters required active social exchange. In this context, the institution *sabla* played a significant role. The *shūra* 'consultation' process, so central to the modern institutional and political development of the Sultanate, having culminated in the formation of the bicameral Majlis Oman (the Oman Council), has its roots in the Omani tradition of consensus-building (*ijmā'*) through communal consultation and daily exchange of news and views over coffee and dates as customarily practised in the *sabla* of a quarter, a tribe, or a tribal leader. Women on the other hand were firmly integrated into a network of regular and reciprocal visits to neighbours and relatives. Everyone would bring her thermos filled with coffee, a container with dates and sometimes other sweets and the assembled women would take turns drinking coffee and having dates from each of the other women. The importance of reciprocal sharing of coffee and dates even features in late 19th-century scholar Nur al-Din al-Salimi's legal compendium *Jawābāt* (2010: 359).

A critical institution for a *ḥāra* community's well-being and social cohesion are religious endowments, *waqf*, pl. *wuqūf*, where the proceeds of a palm garden, individual plots or palm trees, or *falaj* water shares were donated by their owners for a variety of communal purposes, such as the maintenance of mosques, schools, communal paths and cemeteries, procurement of coffee for hospitality in the *sabla*, wood for the preparation of the festive roast in the village oven, *tannūr*, and a range of further purposes. Houses or rooms in houses were also endowed for specific purposes, such as a room in Misfat Al Abriyin for the communal preparation and storage of date vinegar, and another one as a storage place for shepherds. As was the case in major Arab cities (Raymond 2008: 787), the institution *waqf* also played a crucial role in the functioning of the smaller communities of Omani *ḥārāt*. Following Peters' (1990) argument, it may be proposed that endowments constituted pious acts as much as they served the redistribution of wealth within the community. *Wuqūf* therefore represent a major element of communal solidarity and are spatially firmly anchored in a *ḥāra* and its orchards and water system.

These institutions helped shape social interaction in the communities of the oasis settlements and are the basis of the identity and social cohesion-strengthening effect of the settlement quarter on its residents. It was reinforced by the relative self-reliance of the *falaj* communities, under the decentralised Ibadi system of ruling the country, the emphasis on regular consultation, *shūra*, and the lack of a comprehensive administrative apparatus (Valeri 2009: 54), which left the maintenance of the economic infrastructure in the hands of the individual communities (Wilkinson 1980). Omani jurisprudents did encourage communities to follow local customs (Bandhopadhyay – Mershen 2022) and expressed their preference for local governance (Büssow *et al.* 2023: 104). Communities' considerable independence and responsibility was associated with the interdependence of its members and their complementary skills and their "reliance on their own social, economic and spiritual resources" (Dutton 1998: 8). This situation accorded with the Omani Imamate's principles. The Imam, in the first place being a spiritual and political leader (Valeri 2009: 45) had no standing army at his disposal but relied on the consensus of the tribal leaders and, whenever required, their armed tribal forces. Each town and quarter had to organise its own defences. Walis were assisted by a small number of guards, *'askar* (Valeri 2009; Sachedina 2013: 99) were appointed for the larger towns.

Until the wide-ranging transformations of the Omani state and society in the 1970s, Omani oasis towns' residential quarters were thus characterised by tightly knit communities where close cooperation in matters of everyday life, such as the organisation of the *falaj* maintenance and water distribution, was imperative and reflected in the spatial fabric and composition of a quarter's private and communal elements.

Omani *ḥārāt* during the *nahḍa*

Into the mid-20th century seafaring, agriculture, pastoralism and fishing had provided the economic lifeline of the Sultanate of Oman. Urban development in the interior has been associated with the oasis economy, a mixed agro-pastoral system mostly relying on the complex *falaj* irrigation system. This economic and cultural backbone of inland Oman started to lose its pre-eminence in the latter half of the 20th century (Luedeling – Buerkert 2010; Al Shueli 2015: 51). Following the discovery of oil and gas in Oman in the 1950s, the increasing importance of the hydrocarbon sector since the 1960s, and the onset of the Omani *nahḍa* 1970, a completely new set of livelihoods and employment opportunities started to emerge.

The swift opening and modernisation of Oman was achieved through the establishment of a centralised state with a modern administrative apparatus, a police force and an army. The development of modern infrastructure, including road systems, power grid and water supply, schools and hospitals extended to all areas of Oman. The country's tribes and their leaders were incorporated into the evolving new administrative structure by the employment of sheikhs and other notables as governmental advisors and in administrative positions (Valeri 2009: 153), which meant that they were often relocating to the capital area.

Although the intention was to develop the towns in the hinterland as secondary centres while the single growth hub was in the capital area, due to an initial lack of coordinated planning, the towns of inner Oman still "belonged to different worlds" (Scholz 2012: 12–14, 403–405, 461) and the main focus of modern development and employment opportunities was on the capital Muscat. The return of a huge number of Omanis who had previously emigrated to other Gulf countries and beyond was one of the factors leading to the rapid increase of population (Grandmaison 2000: 35). Urbanisation reached 71.7% of the total population in 2010 (Al Jabri 2014: 145) compared to a mere 30% in 1970 (Benkari 2017: 147).

Profound changes swiftly impacted rural areas too. With pronounced migration from rural to urban areas (Benkari 2017: 147), Dutton's study (Dutton 2009) for rural areas between Ibri in Ad Dhahirah and Al Khaburah in Al Batinah North points out that as early as the year 1974, 74% of the adult males were away working elsewhere. The capital area's population on the contrary started to rise at a rapid pace. With job migration toward the capital area and other urban centres ongoing, the resulting imbalance between urban and rural populations has been accelerating. By 2010 the urban population had grown to 71.7% of the total population compared to the rural population's drop to 28.3% (Al Jabri 2014: 145). The latter has since seen a steady decline down to 12.25% in 2022 (Trading Economics 2024).

The job migration of men from rural areas (Oman Observer 2017) previously enrolled in farming their land was a major factor in the disintegration of the "social framework of village life and the decline of oasis agriculture" (Wilkinson 1980). This was followed by abandonment of agricultural land or its conversion into residential land, and the replacement of Omani farmers by expat labourers unfamiliar with the complex socio-cultural and technological mechanisms on which the *falaj* oases thrive (Wilkinson 1980;

Fig. 4: Storage jars kept in a house in the abandoned quarter in Al Baks, Wilayat Al Khabura.

Buerkert – Schlecht 2019: 504; Bandyopadhyay – Mershen 2022). These socio-economic factors are at least partially at fault for the deterioration of many Omani *aflāj* (Al Ghafiri 2018), of which 24% are classified as dead (MRMEWR 2001).

The rapid disintegration of the rural communities created a vacuum in the subsequently mostly abandoned *ḥārāt*. They lay dormant, apart from some ephemeral or secondary uses such as storage (Fig. 4) or labourer accommodation (Fig. 5), and were to be filled with new meaning and purpose only much later and under changed circumstances.

Yet notwithstanding the extent of labour migration and the enormity of rural transformation, the prevailing social structures implicated unwavering bonds between migrants and their relatives and hometowns, *al-bilād*, in the interior.

Although no respective census data sets are available at the National Center for Statistics and Information, it is a familiar fact, described at some length for the Al Sharqiyah region (Hoek 1998: 136–139), that much of the rural out-migration to urban centres (*cf.* Oman Observer 2017), particularly concerning the first generation of job migrants (Al Jabri 2014: 145), is in the form of male commuters who leave their dependents in the countryside and stay in the capital during the week, returning to their family homes in *al-bilād* for the weekend and holidays. The cyclic migration pattern made possible thanks to improved infrastructure and mobility (for example Bontenbal 2016) manifests itself conspicuously in the high volume of traffic to and from Muscat on Thursday afternoons and Sunday mornings, respectively. The higher cost of living in the capital area coupled with the strong social affiliation in the hometown has always been an important argument for keeping the family home in the village and becoming a weekend commuter. Even for families who have

Fig. 5: Former family home in Misfat Al Abriyin, now used as accommodation for expatriate farm workers. Some of their belongings, including a festive outfit, are hung from pegs on the wall.

settled in the capital area, the link to *al-bilād* usually remains strong, and long weekends or holidays are usually spent there in the bosom of one's family.

While the oasis towns were feeling the impacts of rural–urban migration, they too saw modernisation developments in the form of modern physical and social infrastructure and new districts on flat ground outside the old oasis centres taking over all central functions (Scholz 2012: 406). Although in many *ḥārāt* there had been initial attempts toward modernising the mudbrick dwellings, such as plastering them with cement and equipping them with power and water tanks (Mershen *et al.* 2025), eventually many of these practices proved incompatible with the mudbrick construction. When inhabitants moved into new dwellings, the old houses were often repurposed as storage space or accommodation for a family's agricultural labourers, or rented out to expatriate craftsmen.

With Royal Oman Police upholding law and order across the sultanate's territory, *ḥārāt* were relieved of their former defensive function. Had their compact urban morphology hitherto been advantageous for the safety of their inhabitants, the principle of limited access and narrow alleys proved disadvantageous to the fast-paced development of vehicular traffic.

New, demographically heterogeneous residential areas (Richthofen 2016; Al Belushi – Al Hooti 2023) that were created since the *nahḍa* and the development of the nation-state contrasted with the *ḥāra* as a tribal and independent urban entity. The latter henceforth had no role in the young nation-state (Klinger 2021: 163). Under the system of land entitlement, which since 1972 has been stipulated by a series of Royal Decrees (Al Shueili 2015: 121, 395), citizens were allocated building plots, distributed by lottery, in new residential areas planned on previously undeveloped land. The urban morphology changed dramatically with the tightly knit urban fabric with its shaded alleys being replaced by low building density, walled individual compounds and wide and regular street grids.

Organic urban development based on local customs and social structure, and rules and regulations focusing on avoidance of neighbourly conflict and harm, gave way to nationwide urban planning procedures such as prescription of set-back lines of buildings from the plot's front, and rear and side boundaries. In consequence, the inward-looking and mostly attached mansions of the old *ḥārāt* were replaced by freestanding villa-type dwellings built from concrete and oriented toward the outside (Gaube – Gangler 2012: 321).

To achieve the grand transformation from a tribally organised society to a nation-state that included all Omani tribes and population groups where all citizens had a strong national identity and where national unity was based on a unique Omani culture that sits above all ethnic, religious and regional differences (Al Azri 2013: 48–49), Sultan Qaboos rolled out a programme of fast-track economic, infrastructural and social development. Omani school curricula were considered instrumental in the process of fostering such national unity, through heritage education as part of social studies, as formulated by the Ministry of Education in 1978 in its philosophy to guide the educational system and curricula development (Al Maamari 2014). They sought to develop a generic heritage understanding emphasising the importance of the "unique 'Omani national culture'" to serve the goals of national unity and identity (Al Azri 2013: 48) rather than tribal or local identities. Similarly, the focus of religious instruction at the schools and of Friday sermons centrally prepared by the Ministry of Endowment and Religious Affairs was on non-sectarian Islam, rather than Ibadi or Sunni, or Shi'i Islam (Limbert 2010: 91: Eickelman 1987, Valeri 2009: 127). This strategy contributed to forging an "increased sense of national identification" (Uzi 2016: 79; Chatty 1996). The new administrative regions, understood "as culturally differentiated and homogeneous entities" that allow the nation to identify itself as the sum of these geographically delimited cultures, also had a unifying impact on cultural and religious references (Valeri 2009: 146). According to the same author (2009: 245), the regional administrative divisions brought about new regional, rather than tribal, solidarities and identities.

A subsequent recalibration of heritage allegiance may be illustrated by a recent quote from an article in the Oman Observer English Daily (Oman Observer 2024). Elaborating on the opening of a restored section of the town wall around Harat Al 'Aqr and Nizwa Fort and Castle, achieved by local actors, the project is said to have become "a role model that will inspire future generations to preserve the rich heritage of Ad Dakhiliyah Governorate".

Changing perceptions of the *ḥāra* during the early 21st century

The beginning of the Omani Renaissance in the 1970s was marked by a concerted and successful effort to modernize the infrastructure and improve the standard of living of its citizens. Although awareness of local architectural traditions and their potential to contribute to the modern urban development of the Sultanate had already been articulated during a 1973 development workshop, following an earlier visit by Egyptian architect Hassan Fathy (Cain *et al.* 1975: preface), initial efforts of Omani built heritage protection focused primarily on the preservation and restoration of the monumental architecture of forts, castles and towers. Strategically positioned to create a strong defensive system, they are a defining element of the Omani landscape (Groves 2010: 20). Understood to embody "the will of the population and the rulers to defend their territory against raids and attacks from hostile tribes or foreign intruders" (Korn 2008: 118), forts and castles symbolize past greatness and "promoted the concept of a shared cultural identity" (Al Belushi 2008). As a result, dozens of forts, castles and other historical buildings, such as gates, markets and mosques have been restored and opened to the public.

Initial interest in traditional Omani settlements and their architecture (for example Cain *et al.* 1975; Bonnenfant – Al Harthi 1977) gained momentum since the mid-1990s and was encouraged by academic research and discourse (Bandyopadhyay 2004; Mershen 1998; Gaube – Gangler 2012). In 2009, the Ministry of Heritage and Tourism (formerly the Ministry of Heritage and Culture), presiding over the Committee for the Registration and Protection of Historic Settlements in Oman, initiated a process to record, document and protect this vast historical resource. The first phase of the project, which included the registration of over 1,000 *ḥārāt* and their classification as "well-preserved", "semi-sustainable" or "ruinous quarters", was concluded in 2009 (Ministry of Heritage and Culture 2009). Selected quarters were documented, management plans drafted

(Mahrouqi, this vol.), and extensive restoration works carried out in Harat Al Bilad in Manah and Harat Al Jami' in Adam. With the promulgation of the Cultural Heritage Law in 2019 replacing the 1980 National Heritage Protection Law (Al Belushi – Al Hooti 2003), "traditional villages", i.e. *ḥārāt*, were for the first time explicitly recognized as a category of built heritage, thus achieving legal status.

Propelled by the Oman Vision 2040 and the Oman National Spatial Strategy, along with the associated Regional Spatial Strategies developed in close coordination with the Oman Vision 2040 between 2017 and 2020, the government is emphasising regional opportunities and responsibilities. It pursues a process of decentralization where "governorates will gain ever greater autonomy in the management of their affairs, both in the determination of their respective economic and social destinies and in responsibility for the resolution of local tasks and challenges" (MoI 2022). This is coupled with cutting back on the administrative apparatus and the encouragement of the private sector to create more jobs for Omani citizens and incentives to establish small and medium businesses.

The year 2020 was marked by dramatic events, the impact of which should also extend to the discourse and practices involving the abandoned *ḥārāt*. The spread of the new COVID-19 virus and the subsequent global pandemic triggered a staycation trend in Oman that helped promote domestic tourism. The death of Sultan Qaboos bin Said, may he rest in peace, on 10 January of the same year ended an era extending over almost 50 years. Upon his subsequent ascension to the throne, Sultan Haitham bin Tarik emphasized his intent to not only secure the fruits of the Omani *nahḍa* rolled out by his predecessor, but to reinvigorate and renew them in a "renewed renaissance", *al-nahḍa al-'umāniyya al-mutajaddida*. This involved the restructuring of the state apparatus.

The former Ministry of Housing and the Supreme Committee of Urban Planning were combined under the aegis of the new Ministry of Housing and Urban Planning (MoHUP) and entrusted with the implementation of the Oman National Spatial Strategy, and the associated Regional Spatial Strategies for the eleven Omani governorates, that Sultan Haitham bin Tarik endorsed in March 2021. They advocate the bespoke development of each region capitalising on competitive opportunities and locational advantages. Ad Dakhiliyah, the region with the greatest number of abandoned *ḥārāt* (MHC 2009) is envisaged to become a centre of knowledge economy by consolidating its long-standing historical role as a centre for science, culture and knowledge and for environmental and heritage tourism. Its cities shall transform into compact, attractive, well-served modern urban centres, with beautiful traditional oases at their core (MoHUP no date).

Associated with the national spatial strategy is the aim for increased regional self-governance. The decentralized perspective to administration, with additional power given to the governorates to support their respective economic and social ambitions, was implemented with Royal Decree No 36/2022 defining the new structure of governorates and their financial and administrative independence. Some of the key takeaways from ONSS include the promotion of cities' and communities' role in preserving the Omani identity as stressed by H.E. Dr. Al Shueili, Minister of Housing and Urban Planning (interview with Oman TV 2021). ONSS seeks to establish cultural conservation areas in the sense of cultural landscapes. The assets of cultural heritage shall be protected and valued in alignment with the requirements of sustainable urban, social and economic planning. Importantly the strategy also "seeks to formulate an organisation framework to protect and restore those assets, as well as to identify possibilities for their re-investment and management

Fig. 6: The "Old House" is the first private guesthouse set up in Misfat Al Abriyin in 2008.

beside preservation of their Omani identity, by including them in various levels of urban development process."

The Omani *ḥārat* are part of this discourse and a study was commissioned by the Omani State Council's Committee for Culture, Media and Tourism in 2021 on the tourism reuse potential of *ḥārāt*, the findings of which were subsequently endorsed by the Council. This "Old Omani *ḥārāt* and tourism investments" study stressed the *ḥārāt*'s cultural and historical significance and role in identity formation and education, representing an urban and social system that is adapted to the environment and sociocultural setting. In its conclusions, the study called for the development of appropriate legislation, education and training facilities, and for an investment vision for the settlements' restoration, maintenance, and operation as well as for improved cooperation between public and private actors. The *ḥārāt*, it was emphasised, have potential for tourism and income generation and could furthermore constitute an instrument of sustainable urban development. Management plans and guidelines for oasis cities as urban cultural landscapes were said to facilitate the rehabilitation of historic districts as an integral part of ongoing and future urban transformation processes.

New life in old *ḥārāt*

From the perspective of local communities, the early 21st century witnessed the beginnings of a gradually changing perception of the *ḥāra* to a potential economic resource and the first local communal initiatives toward adaptive reuse of buildings in some abandoned *ḥārāt*.

In 2008 a young archaeology graduate adapted his family's old house into a bed and breakfast accommodation, aptly named "The Old House" (Fig. 6). The project's success helped

Fig. 7: Demonstration of traditional household works in Bait Al Safa Museum in Al Hamra.

to change the community's initially unwelcoming attitude towards overnight tourism in their village and over the coming years triggered the establishment of further communal and private tourism enterprises. Similarly, the old quarter of Al Hamra experienced early adaptive reuse initiatives on the part of house owners. The conversion of the sheikhly mansion Bait Al Safa into an ecomuseum[1] (Fig. 7) in the early 2000s was followed by a

1 The term ecomuseum is here understood as a museum focusing on a specific place and the activities of the local population.

further local museum development (Bait Al Jabal), and in 2018 the establishment of the local "Loyal to Harat Al Hamra initiative" aiming at restoring local landmarks, cleaning the *falaj* and oasis pathways, setting up signboards informing about names, age and functions of buildings, establishing a fund for the quarter's reconstruction and spreading cultural awareness. Starting with sporadic initiatives, the development of adaptive predominantly tourism-related reuse of abandoned *ḥārāt* gained momentum in the latter second decade of the 21st century (Biezeveld *et al.* 2023).

Present-day efforts toward revalorisation of many Omani *ḥārāt* either on site or in social media are sustained to a great extent by young generations, such as school children and students taking part in communal cleaning campaigns as part of sports teams, young social media users or influencers as well as entrepreneurs. Omani *ḥārāt* are currently being described as yet "untapped tourist icons" (Jaridat Wujuhat 2023). In some of them, such as Harat Al 'Aqr in Nizwa, Al Hamra, Birkat Al Mawz or Misfat Al 'Abriyin domestic and international tourism are already thriving while residents are equally enjoying the new venues (Fig. 8 and Fig. 9) to meet with friends, the well-lit and tended urban and palm garden areas for evening strolls as well as the emerging new cultural activities offered in the old quarters.

This apparent new interest in the abandoned mudbrick quarters is neither self-evident nor allegeable as a conservative attitude of holding on to tradition and respect for the ancestral quarters. It certainly was not the prevailing attitude when I was taking students out on field trips to abandoned quarters in Manah, Sinaw, Ibra, Al Jabal al Akhdar and elsewhere in the mid-to-late 1990s. While there was curiosity and excitement of discovery on the part of the students, they also felt distant from the abandoned, crumbling remains of dwellings still enclosing many relics of past activities of daily life. In our discussions, they did not display an urge toward the preservation of those *ḥārāt*. On several occasions, I was told that one was grateful to have put those behind oneself and to be living in modern housing facilities with all respective amenities.

Limbert (2010: 15) in the mid-to-late 1990s made similar observations on young Bahlawis' negative attitudes towards the past and certain social practices related to the old quarters. In the 2010s the dilemma of young students commuting between the capital area and their hometowns in the interior was elaborated on by Scott Winer (2015). According to his findings, this commuter model created a duality of values for the students and resulted in identity problems. Many young people from the interior were described as seeing the capital area as an exciting, modern cosmopolitan city where they study and work while they commute back to their families in their hometown on weekends. In this "Muscat Commute", Winer and his interviewee Ahmad Al Mukhaini saw the trigger for conflicting values between the interior of the country and the capital, where young people must try to reconcile tradition and modernity, leading to the schizophrenic situation where at home they conform to the more conservative society, while in Muscat they feel like trendsetters.

Such reconciliation of the conflictive construal of the abandoned mudbrick quarters now appears to be in reach, enabled through their reconfiguration as refurbished, revalorized and smart places, embodying economic resources, entrepreneurial creativity and a young spirit for old *ḥāra*, thus making them once again meaningful to young people who can take ownership of the reconfigured *ḥārāt* as entrepreneurs, employees or as visitors.

Inspired by public discourse on abandoned neighbourhoods, such as a newspaper's online discussion of the *ḥārāt*'s future (Studio Al Roya 2021), state institutions have begun to address

Fig. 8: Wide-ranging tourism offers being advertised in Al 'Aqr, Nizwa.

Fig. 9: Young Omanis enjoying an evening at the Bait Al Sabah coffee shop in Birkat Al Mawz.

Fig. 10: Parts of the old village in Misfat Al Abriyin that are open to tourists alternate with spaces and buildings signposted as private and off-limits to visitors.

them not just as architectural monuments, but as tourism assets and opportunities for local employment and income generation while being valued as cultural heritage and cultural identifiers (State Council 2021). It remains to be seen whether the principles and urban elements inherent in the *ḥārāt* will also establish themselves as an instrument of sustainable urban development in current and future state planning, such as through the integration of *ḥārāt*, date gardens and *falaj* irrigation system in the urban planning framework of the oasis town as a cultural landscape, as already proposed in the Oman National Spatial Strategy.

Perceived disturbance of the privacy of the *ḥāra* (Fig. 10) by the admission of strangers, especially when they were to stay overnight, had been a major obstacle impeding initial attempts and delaying the development of tourism accommodation facilities in places such as Misfat Al Abriyin (personal communication Ahmed Al Abri). The transformation of a *ḥāra* from a closed and exclusive to an open and inclusive place came to be accepted following the success of exemplary adaptive reuse projects in generating income as well as prestige and reputation by showcasing the *ḥāra*'s and its people's history and heritage to the outside world. A study conducted on local residents' perception of tourism conducted in the Ad Dakhiliyah region in the mid-2010s showed an increasing trend toward self-employment, entrepreneurial initiatives as well as private sector employment that goes along with the perception of the economic impacts of tourism as beneficial due to their potential to generate employment and increase business opportunities for local residents. At the same time, the survey revealed residents' overwhelmingly positive perception "with regard to its [tourism's] impact on their socio-cultural beliefs" and the belief "that tourism increases the residents' pride in their local culture" (Malik *et al.* 2017).

Conclusion

The inhabited *ḥārāt* as the centre of inhabitants' daily life, with a complex web of sociocultural and economic practices, had transformed by the late 20th century into ruinous, largely abandoned areas with peripheral secondary reuse of spaces. But despite their perceived marginality, *ḥārāt* remained highly visible, continuing to express tribal presence and historical ownership. The sociocultural significance of the *ḥārāt*'s spatio-material heritage is by association with intangible heritage, traditional institutions, and memories. The collective memory (Halbwachs 1950: 131–139) of historical events and personalities, of one's ancestors and of former social cohesion in the old neighbourhood, invest it with a spirit of place, *genius loci*, as a value communities attribute to the place (Plevoets – Van Cleempoel, 2011) that continues to create bonds with its former inhabitants and their offspring. The collective memory of scholars, sheikhs and judges associated with a quarter, mosque, dwelling, garden and other places, and revered as moral or spiritual role models has remained strong. As an example, the former dwelling and school, Bait Al Qadim of Shaykh Majid Al Abri in Al Hamra may be mentioned. In a newspaper article Al Zaidi describes the presence of the revered sheikh as perceptible in its ruin (Al Zaidi 2017). Commemorative practices (Shub 2020) in the library and museum of another famous sheikh from Al Hamra, Sheikh Mohsin Al 'Abri, include the display not only of photographs and documents relating to Sheikh Mohsin but also a range of personal belongings, such as his spectacles, prayer beads and perfume bottles (Fig. 11). Collective memory and commemoration furthermore figure prominently in videos about individual *ḥārāt*, such as a YouTube video about Al Ghafat (Al Hinai 2016), where the ghosts of long-passed-away

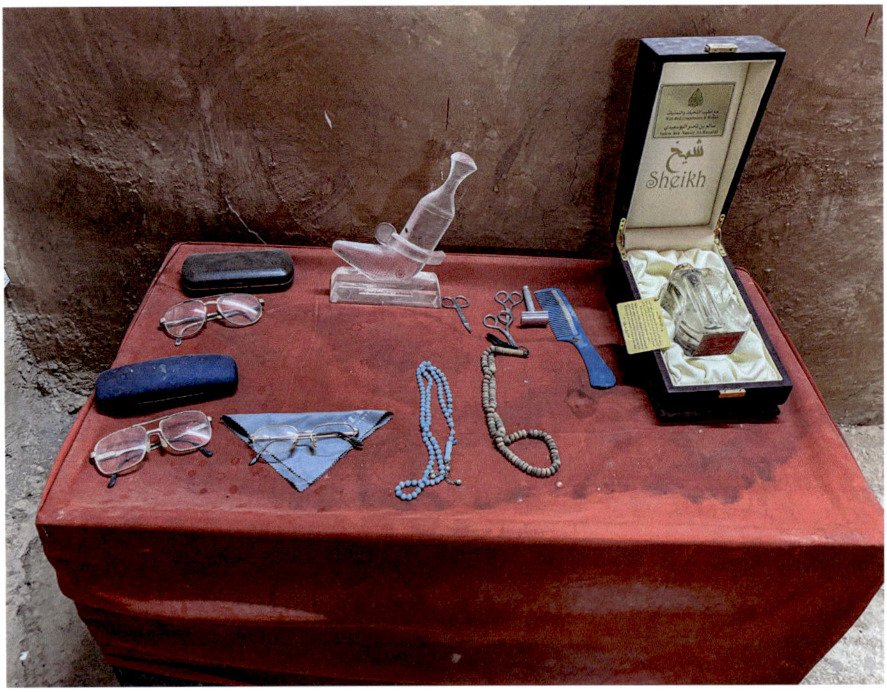

Fig. 11: Spectacles, prayer beads and a perfume bottle from the possession of the late Shaykh Mohsin on display in the Shaykh Mohsin Al 'Abri Library and Museum in Al Hamra.

residents are evoked through photographs and poetry to virtually repopulate the ruins of the quarter.

The association of order, continuity, stability and security transmitted by the memory of familiar surroundings (Halbwachs 1950: 128) even after putting buildings to new uses (Cantacuzino 1975: 263), provides for a group's social cohesion even after their spatial dispersion (Halbwachs 1950: 130). It derives special relevance in periods of uncertainty, such as the recent COVID-19 pandemic, as can be gathered for example from the overriding significance attached to the old, abandoned mudbrick house of the Omani family featured in the 2022 Netflix series "Scattered Barriers" (Scattered Barriers 2022).

In the wake of the modern transformation of the Sultanate and of increasing urbanization of the capital area and beyond, the countryside hometown, *al-bilād*, in the 21st century has not lost its appeal as a preferred retirement option to many of those working in the city. In this context the old *ḥārāt* gain new relevance; they are used as historical points of reference, to reposition oneself in an increasingly urbanized and globalized present. The blend of the intangible spatial framework of collective memory with tangible economic and sociopolitical factors has created a basis for processes of reinvestment into the adaptive reuse of many abandoned *ḥārāt*. Similar to Oman's monumental and highly visible Bronze Age tombs, which have been interpreted as markers of tribal territories and access to natural resources for the Bronze Age communities living "in the shadow of the ancestors" (Cleuziou – Tosi 2007: 132), *ḥārāt* too, continue to connote spatio-material markers of particular groups, their social cohesion, their water and agricultural resources, which recently are evolving into economic resources in their own right.

Fig. 12: Newly developed tourism establishments are booming in Harat Al 'Aqr in Nizwa.

In the late 2010s and 2020s, the Omani *ḥāra* is being reconfigured and revalorised under new parameters where the privacy of the *hāra* metamorphoses into exposure, a place where messages of communal memory and spirit of place address a widened audience, embracing not only the quarter's community but the "others", those which formerly had been outside of the walls (Limbert 2010: 29) and were considered not to belong there. Walls previously protecting residential quarters are opening their gates to outsiders, domestic and international visitors, signifying both an ultimate step of Oman's opening in the context of the renewed *nahḍa* and the assertion of local communities' spatial presence and initiatives. The perception of the *ḥāra*'s new functionality as an economic resource

Fig. 13: A ruined house in Harat Al 'Aqr, Nizwa, being offered for sale. The redevelopment of the old *ḥāra* in Al 'Aqr has seen property prices shooting up.

(Fig. 12 and Fig. 13) and its character transformation from a place restricted for the use of its residents to a public arena showcasing local cultural heritage and its association with important historic personalities furthermore serves the perpetuation of tribal groups' territoriality and control.

Far from conflicting with it, the valorisation of the *ḥāra* through its newly acquired significance as an economic asset and potential source of income generation is both reinforced by and reinforcing the sociocultural significance of its reconfigured manifestation. Names and designations, past uses and functions of a *ḥāra*'s architectural and spatial elements or connections to historic personalities, which formerly were transmitted orally, are now publicised and visualised through labelling, wayfinding signage and musealisation.

With primary and secondary uses of space replaced by tertiary uses in the form of community spaces, heritage accommodation, museums, coffeeshops and similar, the revalorized *ḥārāt* 2.0 are gaining a new centrality as productive economic resources, allowing young generations of Omanis to relate to and take ownership of their ancestors' quarters which, reinvested with pride as national cultural heritage, serve as markers of national and regional identity.

References

Al Azri, K. M. 2013
Social and gender inequality in Oman. The power of religious and political tradition, London/New York.

Al Belushi, M. 2008
Managing Oman's archaeological resources: Historical perspectives, *Public Archaeology* 7/3, 149–173. DOI: 10.1179/175355308X383982

Al Belushi, M. – Al Hooti, N. 2023
Preserving the past, shaping the present: Insights on Oman's built heritage and its identity, *European Journal of Architecture and Urban Planning* 2/3. DOI: 10.24018/ejarch.2023.2.3.31

Al Ghafri, A. 2018
Overview about the aflaj of Oman [paper presented at the International Symposium of Khattaras and Aflaj].

Al Hamawi, Y. 1977
Muʿjam al-buldān 5, Beirut.

Al Hinai, N. 2016
Baldat al-Ghafāt [YouTube video, https://www.youtube.com/watch?v=pYCxbQ-gJNQ, accessed 12.12.2022].

Al Jabri, H. 2014
The planning and urban design of liveable public open spaces in Oman: Case study of Muscat [PhD thesis, Heriot-Watt University].

Al Kuddami, Abu Sa'id Muhammad bin Said bin Muhammad bin Said 1975
Al-jāmiʿ al-mufīd min aḥkām Abī Saʿīd 3, Muscat.

Al Maamari, S. 2014
Education for developing a global Omani citizen: Current practices and challenges, *Journal of Education and Training Studies* 2/3, 108–117. DOI: 10.11114/jets.v2i3.399

Al Maqdisi, Muammad bin Ahmad Shams al-Din 1906
Aḥsan al-taqāsīm fī ma'rifat al-aqālīm, Leiden.

Al Salimi, Nur al-Din 'Abdallah bin Humaid 2010
Jawābāt al-Imām al-Sālimī 5, 'Abdallah bin Muhammad bin Abdallah al-Salimi (ed.). Biddiya: Maktabat al-Imām al-Sālimī, Biddiya.

Al Shueili, K. 2015
Towards a sustainable urban future in Oman: Problem and process analysis (Muscat as a case study) [PhD thesis, the Glasgow School of Art].

Al Zaidi, K. 2017
Ḥārat al-Ḥamrā' al-qadīma. Ayna taraḥḥala al-sukkānu?, *Al Watan Newspaper*, 22.01.2017. https://alwatan.com/details/168229

Bandyopadhyay, S. 2004
Ḥārat al-Bilād (Manah): Tribal pattern, settlement structure and architecture, *The Journal of Omani Studies* 13, 183-263.

Bandyopadhyay, S. – Mershen, B. 2022
Falaj communities in Oman: A case for local governance? *Ibadī* legal rulings and spatial and ethnohistorical observations, *Journal of Material Cultures in the Muslim World* 3/1, 6–47. DOI:10.1163/26666286-12340028

Benkari, N. 2017
Urban development in Oman: An overview, in: C. A. Brebbia – J. Longhurst – E. Marco –C. Booth (eds) *Sustainable Development and Planning IX*, Southampton, 143–156.

Buerkert, A. – Schlecht, E. 2019
Agriculture in the Western Hajar Mountains, in: B. Mershen – S. Al Saqri (eds), *The Mountains of Oman, An illustrated reference to nature and society* 1, Hildesheim, 491–505.

Bonnenfant, P. – Bonnenfant, G. – Al Harthi, S. 1977
Architecture and social history at Mudayrib, *The Journal of Oman Studies* 3, 107–135

Bontenbal, M. 2016
Population, migration and urbanisation in Oman, in: S. Nebel – A. von Richthofen (eds) *Urban Oman: Trends and perspectives of urbanisation in Muscat Capital Area*, Berlin.

Büssow, J. – Hoffmann-Ruf, M. – Al Saqri, N. 2023
Al-Sūr al-Muḥīṭ. The city wall of Bahla as a case study for the organisation of communal tasks in central Oman on the eve of modern state administration, 1967-1977, Bonner Islamstudien 47, Berlin.

Cain, A. – Afshar, F. – Norton, J. 1975
Oman: The problems and potentials of the indigenous built environment in a developing country [report Development Workshop].

Cantacuzino, S. 1975
New uses for old buildings, New York.

Chatty, D. 1996
Local administration and Harasis tribal authority in the Sultanate of Oman, *Nomadic Peoples* 38, 137–150.

Cleuziou, S. – Tosi, M. 2007
In the shadow of the ancestors. The prehistoric foundations of the early Arabian civilization in Oman, Muscat.

Dutton, R. W. 2009
Changing rural systems in Oman – The Khabura Project, London/New York.

Eickelman, D. F. 1987
Ibadism and the sectarian perspective, in: B. R. Pridham (ed.) *Oman. Economic, social and strategic developments*, London, 31–50.

Gaube, H. – Gangler, A. 2012
Transformation processes in oasis settlements of Oman, Muscat.

Halbwachs, M. 1980
The collective memory, New York.

Hoek, C. W. 1998
Shifting sands. Social-economic development in al-Sharqiyah region, Oman, Nijmegen.

Jaridat Wujuhat 2023
Al-ḥārāt al-qadīma fī 'Umān. Aikūnāt sīyaḥīyya ghair mustathmira! *Jaridat Wujuhat*, 11.12.2023. https://wejhatt.com/?p=82985

Klinger, T. 2022
L'Oman contemporain. Aménagement du territoire et l'identité nationale, Berlin.

Le Cour Grandmaison, B. 2000
Le Sultanat d'Oman, Paris.

Luedeling, E. – Buerkert, A. 2010
Typology of oases in northern Oman, in: A. Buerkert – E. Schlecht (eds), *Oases of Oman. Livelihood systems at the crossroads*, Muscat, 26–29.

Limbert, M. 2010
In the time of oil – Piety, memory and social life in an Omani town, Standford.

Malik, M. – Al Rawabi, T. – Al Kimyani, N. – Al Hadrami, S. 2017
Residents perception of tourism impacts in Ad Dhakhiliyah region of the Sultanate of Oman, *Ottoman Journal of Tourism and Management Research* 2/3, 119–134. DOI:10.26465/ojtmr.2017239498

Mershen, B. – Kanditt, J. – Schmidt-Lux, T. – Döpper, S. – Biezeveld, I. 2025
Ḥārāt al Hamra: The journey from an Oasis town to a 'Heritage Village', *Journal of Arabian Studies*. DOI: 10.1080/21534764.2024.2448042

MHC (Ministry of Heritage and Culture) 2009
Mashrū' tauthīq al-ḥārāt al- 'umānīyya. Al-marḥala al-awalī – ḥaṣr al-ḥārāt, Muscat [report].

MoI (Ministry of Information) 2022
Oman 2022, Muscat.

MoHUP (Ministry of Housing and Urban Development) no date
Features of the Urban Strategy 2040 [report]. https://www.housing.gov.om/cmsapi/files/content/information_center/Features%20of%20the%20Urban%20Strategy%202040%20.pdf

MRMEWR (Ministry of Regional Municipalities, Environment and Water Resources) 2001
Aflaj inventory project summary report [unpublished report].

Oman Observer 2017
Urban migration leaves rural towns empty, *Oman Observer* 18.10.2017. www.omanobserver.om/article/70743/Opinion/urban-job-migration-leaves-rural-towns-empty.

Oman Observer 2024
Restored Al Aqur wall now pride of Nizwa, *Oman Observer* 15.01.2024. https://www.omanobserver.om/article/1148249/features/restored-al-aqur-wall-now-pride-of-nizwa

Oman TV 2021
Al-strātījīyyah al-waṭanīyya li'l-tanmiyya al-'umrānīyya, interview with Dr. Khalfan Al Shueili,

Minister of Housing and Urban Planning, *Oman TV*, 16.03.2021. https://www.youtube.com/watch?v=Hz5hlekZUM0

Peters, E. L. 1990
The power of sheikhs, in: J. Goody – E. Marx (eds), *The Bedouin of Cyrenaica. Studies in personal and corporate power*, Cambridge, 112–137.

Plevoets, B. – van Cleempoel, K. 2011
Adaptive reuse as a strategy towards conservation of cultural heritage: A literature review, in: C. A. Brebbia – L. Binda (eds), *Structural Repairs and Maintenance of Heritage Architecture XII*, Southampton, 155–163. DOI: 10.2495/STR110131

Rabi, U. 2016
The Sultanate Oman, in: U. Rabi (ed.), *Tribes and states in a changing Middle East*, London, 79–94.

Raymond, A. 2008
The management of the city, in: S. K. Jayyusi – R. Holod – A. Petruccioli – A. Raymond (eds), *The City in the Islamic World* 2, Leiden, 775–793.

Sachedina, A. 2013
Of living traces and revived legacies: Unfolding futures in the Sultanate of Oman [PhD thesis, University of California, Berkley].

Scattered Barriers 2022
Netflix mini-series "Scattered Barriers". https://www.imdb.com/title/tt19284102/

Scholz, F. 2014
Muscat then and now: Geographical sketch of a unique Arab town, Muscat/Berlin.

Shub, M. 2020
Cultural assessment of commemorative practices: Methodological aspects, *KnE Social Sciences* 4/11, 138–144. DOI: 10.18502/kss.v4i11.7541

State Council 2021
Al-ḥārāt al-'umānīyya al-qadīma wa taḥadīyyāt al-istithmār al-siyāḥī [report].

Studio Al Roya 2021
Taṭwīr al-qura al-turāthīyah, Studio Al Roya open online discussion, 31.01.2021. www.youtube.com/watch?v=Krc722jUeic&feature=youtu.be.

Trading Economics 2024
Oman – Rural Population – 2024 Data 2025 Forecast 1960-2022 Historical, accessed 28.01.2024. https://tradingeconomics.com/oman/rural-population-wb-data.html

Valeri, M. 2009
Oman: Politics and society in the Qaboos State, New York.

von Richthofen, A. 2016
Parameters of urban expansion in Oman, in: S. Nebel – A. von Richthofen (eds) *Urban Oman: Trends and perspectives of urbanisation in Muscat Capital Area*, Berlin, 101–118.

Wilkinson, J. C. 1980
Changes in the structure of village life in Oman, in: T. Niblock (ed.), *Social and economic development in the Arab Gulf*, London/Canberra, 122–134.

Winer, S. J. 2015
The Muscat commute. A young generation's journey between tradition and modernity, internet blog post for the Arab Gulf States Institute in Washington. https://agsiw.org/the-muscat-commute-a-young-generations-journey-between-tradition-and-modernity/

Harat Al ʿAqr in Nizwa and Three Artistic Traditions

Soumyen Bandyopadhyay and Claudia Briguglio[1]

Introduction

This chapter is concerned with two important and interrelated issues: the study of settlement structure and evolution, or morphology, as a critical means of understanding traditional settlements in the Arabian Peninsula, and its importance to the conservation of historic oasis settlements. It focuses on the settlement quarter of Harat Al ʿAqr, the historic core of the ancient Omani oasis of Nizwa in Ad Dakhiliyah region. The physical structure of historic oases and their constituent settlement quarters have received limited attention, and consequently, the study of their form and transformation over time remain poorly studied and understood. Our knowledge of how historic settlements of the Arabian Peninsula have been shaped by physical, socio-political and cultural forces thus remains patchy at best.

The detrimental impact of this gap in knowledge can be observed in the conservation approaches adopted for historic settlement quarters, which are often oblivious of their morphological characteristics. Settlement morphology, as well as the study of the transformation of spatial types of buildings, provide a resilient basis for identifying the unique characteristics and significances – their continuities and the apparent idiosyncratic complexities – resulting from divergent and often contradictory socio-political forces. Understanding these leads to the identification of distinctive values – historical, cultural, social, aesthetic, scientific, and so on – that require protection (*cf.* the Burra Charter,

1 The chapter draws on several seasons of fieldwork undertaken under various projects funded by the Omani government and UK funding bodies. Extensive fieldwork was undertaken and data collected during the *al-ʿAqr Traditional Quarter Development Project* in 2004 with Consulting Engineering Services (CES), commissioned by the Ministry of Regional Municipalities and Water Resources (MRMWR). Extensive survey of the decorated prayer niches was conducted through the Arts and Humanities Research Board (AHRB, now Council, AHRC) funded project, *The Decorated Mihrabs (Prayer Niches) of Central Oman* (2003-4). More recent fieldwork took place during the *Earthen Architecture Course* (*EAC*) at Al ʿAqr, a visit supported by the Getty Conservation Institute (2022). Valuable information was provided by Ali Hamood Al Mahrooqi, which drew on his postgraduate research on Harat al ʿAqr, and Omar Sulaiman al Sabahi, a resident of Nizwa involved with the tourism industry. Henry Rogers generously allowed the use of valuable photographs taken during survey of the Omani Interior in 1960, and John Warr kindly donated photographs taken in the early-1970s to the ArCHIAM research centre, now at the University of Liverpool.

in: S. Döpper – B. Mershen – J. Kanditt – I. Biezeveld – T. Schmidt-Lux (eds) 2025, *Mudbrick Settlements of the Oman Peninsula. Inhabited – Abandoned – Re(dis)covered,* Leiden: Sidestone Press, 91–118.

Australia ICOMOS 2013). Beyond conservation, if future expansion of historic cores were to achieve a degree of resonance with the past, such interventions within and around historic sites must learn from the consistencies and contradictions, and develop methodologies attuned to their context.

Today there is much ongoing heritage tourism at Harat Al ʿAqr; resulting from very welcome bottom-up stakeholder initiatives, it is quickly transforming the fabric of the settlement. However, a management plan based on robust historical knowledge, carefully considered implementation approaches, and appropriate regulatory mechanisms are needed to manage heritage. While change is inevitable and certainly also desirable, the processes of managing change are critical to the protection of the values and significances they once held, and continue to hold, for the past, present and future communities and individuals. Settlement transformations often leave behind physical traces or fragments of earlier configurations within the fabric of the settlement. These preserve evidence of earlier form and structure connected with older social, political and cultural status. In Harat Al ʿAqr, in the absence of research prompting their safeguarding, the recent enthusiastic touristic initiatives have sadly led to the unfortunate disappearance of some of those traces and fragments.

This chapter aims to develop a detailed understanding of the urban morphological characteristics of Harat Al ʿAqr, with a view to contributing more immediately to the ongoing heritage tourism effort there, as well as developing a methodological approach for Oman and the Arabian Peninsula. In doing so, two key problems will be addressed. The first is an over-emphasis on the subsistence economy status of Omani oasis settlements, pre-1970, a discourse that has diverted attention away from the social production of *urban artifacts* and artistic traditions that may have impacted or shaped the historic quarters. Urban artifacts, following Rossi, are collective works of art – those indispensable components of a settlement which are characterised by their rich history, distinctive form and individuality (Rossi 1982). Periodic accumulation of wealth took place under strong Ibadi-Islamic imamate rule,[2] with some centralisation of land, resources and infrastructure; however, its impact on the "everyday" built environment of the settlement quarters remained undocumented beyond the attention given to a handful of forts and castles that resulted from it. This chapter assesses how artistic production that resulted from such wealth accumulation under the Ibadi state at three different periods were either instrumental in or intrinsic to the evolution of Al ʿAqr.

Secondly, while since the early Islamic period Nizwa and Al ʿAqr were the centre of Ibadi religious learning alongside a small number of ancient oasis settlements, how this culture translated into more tangible urban or artistic production has remained poorly explored. We argue that this resulted from an arrangement of social production between the Ibadi state and the local community, the latter comprised of diverse tribal groups. Associated with this is the tendency to regard the Ibadi imamate as an introspective culture focused on an inland "island" territory, away from the maritime world of the Indian Ocean. Thus, this chapter demonstrates how the three artistic traditions also indicate a strong

2 Ibadism emerged from the political turmoil that engulfed the Islamic community in the seventh century and was introduced into Oman in the late Umayyad period by the many Omani-Ibadi personalities active in Basrah. The Ibadi imamate evolved as a supra-tribal state and represented a delicate balance between tribal aspirations and the power and purity of Ibadi-Islamic philosophy (Wilkinson 1987).

and longstanding maritime tradition that has always impacted the geographical core of the Oman Peninsula.

We consider three important phases of settlement development at Al 'Aqr, linked to three key imamate phases and associated artistic and architectural traditions. The first is the often-ignored struggle to reestablish the imamate between the mid-fifteenth and late-sixteenth centuries, especially during the period of the Nizwan imam, Muhammad bin Ismail (1500/01–1536). It saw the revival of the decorated *miḥrāb* (prayer niche; pl. *maḥārīb*) tradition with the introduction of Chinese porcelain inserts, including at Masjid Al Shawadhinah in Al 'Aqr. The next is during the reign of the Ya'ariba imam, Saif bin Sultan in the later part of the 17th century, when significant rebuilding of the defensive wall and town reorganisation took place in close collaboration with the local community, funded by wealth from expanding Indian Ocean trade. The third tradition is the least known; it emerges in the early Al Bu Said phase during the rule of Imam Ahmed bin Said (mid-1740s). We explore the likely maritime origin of a timber-crafting tradition that emerged within the newly built Al Bu Said houses and its spread across central Oman.

Harat Al 'Aqr

Nizwa is located approximately 175 km south of the capital Muscat, bordered by the western section of the Jabal Al Akhdar (Al Hajar Al Gharbi) in the north and the wilayat of Bahla to the west, Izki to the east, and Manah and Adam to the south. Nizwa, Bahla, and Izki form the inner ring of large piedmont settlements, which have played an important politico-cultural role since ancient times. This settlement crescent is connected to a coastal strip of settlements through a major transmontaine route, the Samail Gap. Nizwa is the administrative centre of Ad Dakhiliyah Governorate (*muḥāfaẓah*) as well as the most populous province (*wilāyah*) of the same name (Fig. 1).

Bounded by the Jabal Hallah to the west and the Al Hawrah ridge to the east, the Nizwa oasis has a linear configuration structured around the valley formed by the two wadis, Abyad and Kalbu.[3] The wadis divide the oasis into two parts: Alayat (Upper) Nizwa and Sufalat (Lower) Nizwa. These contain the important and ancient residential quarters of the oasis: Samad Al Kinda in Upper Nizwa, and Harat Al 'Aqr and Saal in Lower Nizwa. The two wadis meet near Al 'Aqr – the main residential quarter of Nizwa, where the main market (*sūq*) and the Friday Mosque (*al-jāmi'*) are located. The old *jāmi'* stood on a promontory within the wadi, and the *sūq* on its southern edge, both in the shadow of the imposing round tower of Nizwa Fort (Husn Al 'Aqr), which was rebuilt in the seventeenth century to adjoin Al 'Aqr. The ancient irrigation systems (*aflāj*, s. *falaj*) for the Nizwa oasis consists of the Falaj Daris, Dawt, Ghantaq, Saali and others, of which Daris is now designated as a UNESCO World Heritage Site (*cf.* Nizwa *aflāj* map, Gaube – Gangler 2012: 242–244; Fig. 2).

The entirely fortified settlement of Al 'Aqr, once studded with 17 towers, occupies a large area of approximately 8.7 hectares, partially defined to the north by the vast expanse of the fort. The northern gate, Bab Al Husn, originally facing the fort entrance, has long since disappeared, although photographic evidence of it exists. However, the eastern (Bab Al Sabah), southern (Bab Al Muthar) and western (Bab Al Sukhbi) gates, all flanked by single towers, exist in various states of preservation. The best preserved is the southern gateway;

3 Wadis are dry water courses which become active during rainfall.

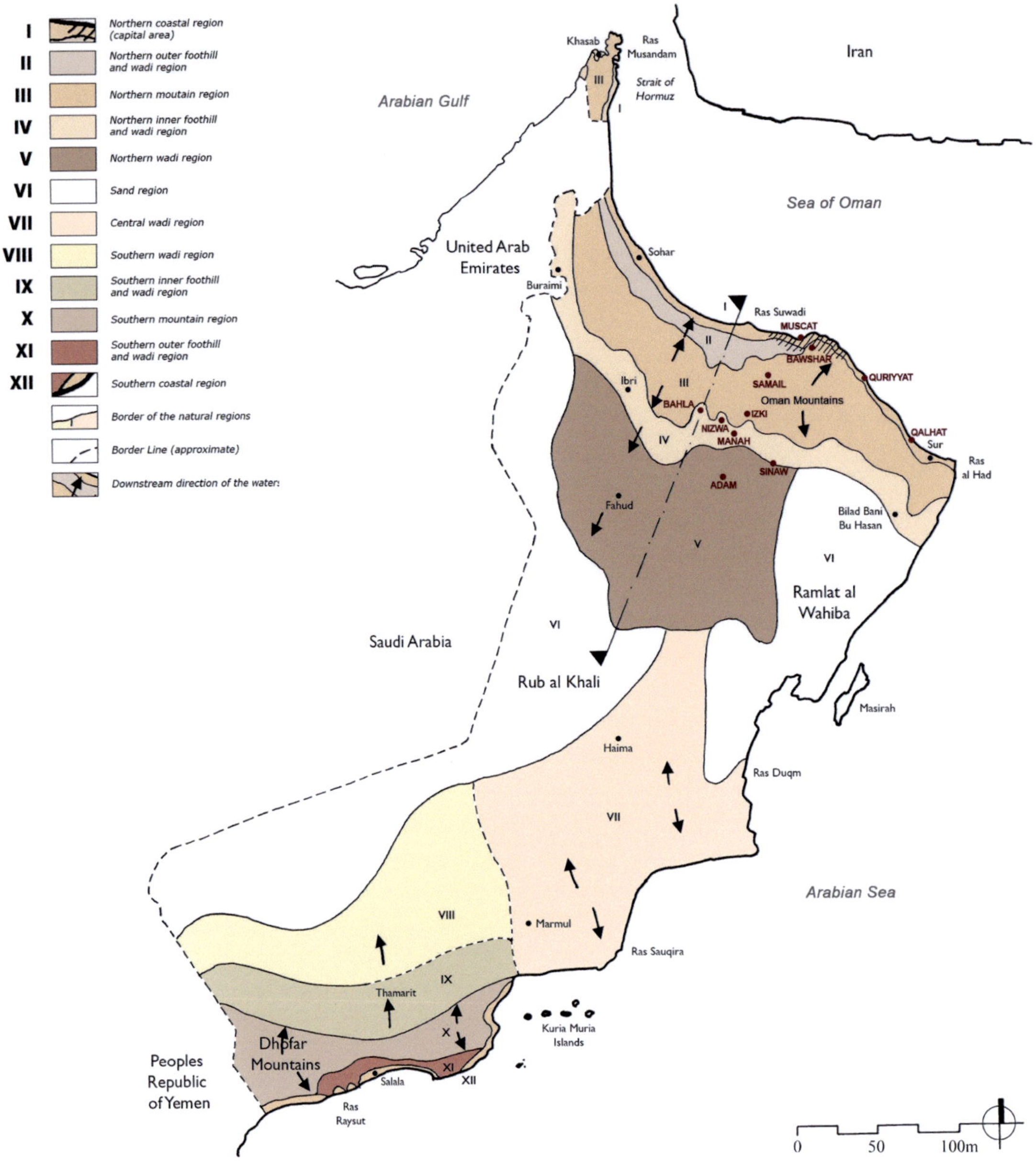
I Northern coastal region (capital area)
II Northern outer foothill and wadi region
III Northern moutain region
IV Northern inner foothill and wadi region
V Northern wadi region
VI Sand region
VII Central wadi region
VIII Southern wadi region
IX Southern inner foothill and wadi region
X Southern mountain region
XI Southern outer foothill and wadi region
XII Southern coastal region
Border of the natural regions
Border Line (approximate)
Downstream direction of the water:
Khasab
Ras Musandam
Strait of Hormuz
Iran
Arabian Gulf
Sea of Oman
United Arab Emirates
Buraimi
Sohar
Ras Suwadi
MUSCAT
BAWSHAR
QURIYYAT
SAMAIL
Ibri
BAHLA
Oman Mountains
NIZWA
IZKI
MANAH
QALHAT
Sur
Ras al Had
SINAW
ADAM
Fahud
Bilad Bani Bu Hasan
Ramlat al Wahiba
Saudi Arabia
Rub al Khali
Masirah
Haima
Ras Duqm
Arabian Sea
Marmul
Ras Sauqira
Thamarit
Kuria Muria Islands
Dhofar Mountains
Peoples Republic of Yemen
Salala
Ras Raysut
0
50
100m

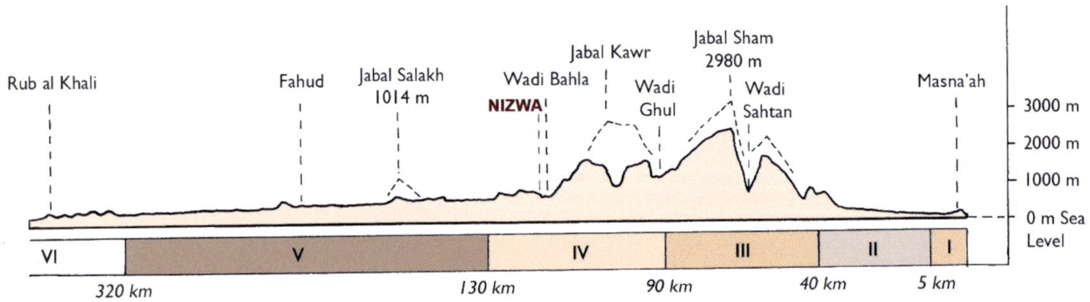
Rub al Khali
Fahud
Jabal Salakh 1014 m
Wadi Bahla
NIZWA
Jabal Kawr
Wadi Ghul
Jabal Sham 2980 m
Wadi Sahtan
Masna'ah
3000 m
2000 m
1000 m
0 m Sea Level
VI
V
IV
III
II
I
320 km
130 km
90 km
40 km
5 km

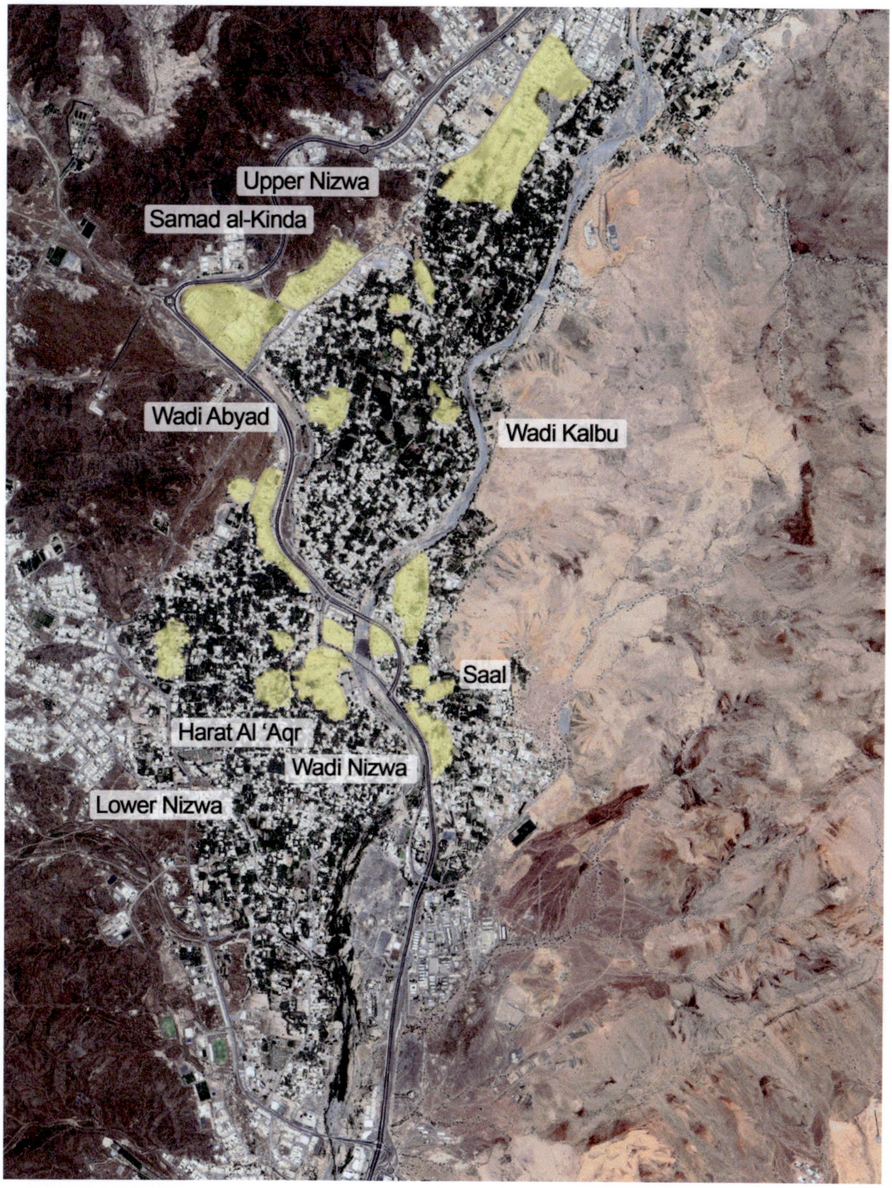

Fig. 2: Map of Nizwa oasis showing the key settlement areas. The important and ancient residential quarters of the oasis are, Samad al-Kinda in Upper Nizwa, and Al ʿAqr and Saal in Lower Nizwa. The two wadis, Abyad and Kalbu, meet north of Al ʿAqr – the main residential quarter of Nizwa, where the fort, main market and the Friday Mosque are located (drawing: Briguglio, after Google Earth, accessed: 20 December, 2024)

(Opposite page) Fig. 1: The six major geographical regions of Oman, and a schematic cross-section through the Oman Mountains close to Nizwa (drawing: ArCHIAM, after Scholz 1978: 6, 8).

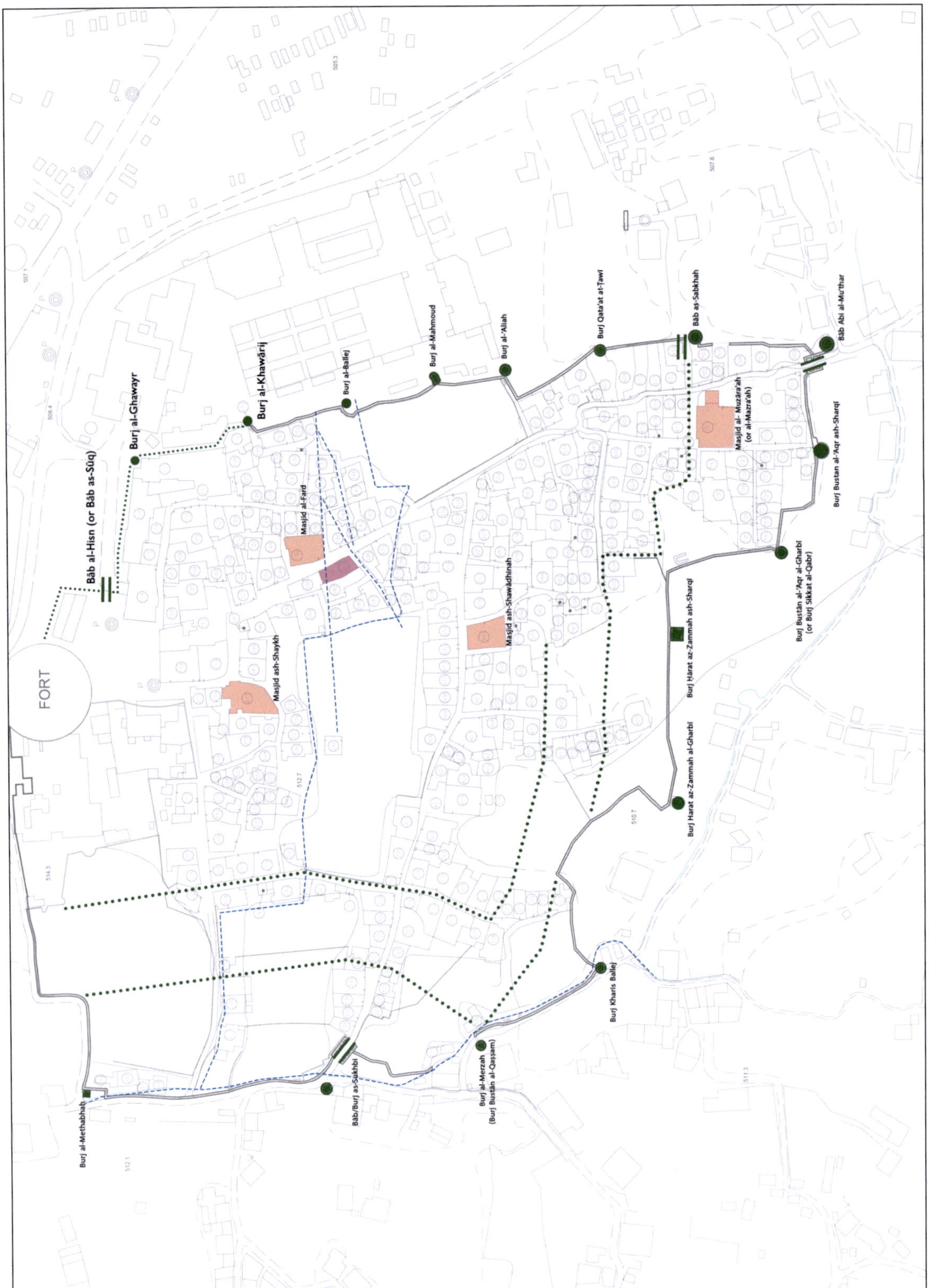
FORT
Bāb al-Hisn (or Bāb as-Sūq)
Burj al-Ghawayr
Burj al-Khawārij
Burj al-Ballej
Burj al-Mahmoud
Burj al-'Aliah
Burj Qata'at at-Tawi
Bāb as-Sabkhah
Bāb Abi al-Mu'thar
Masjid al- Muzāra'ah
(or al-Mazra'ah)
Burj Bustan al-'Aqr ash-Sharqi
Burj Bustān al-'Aqr al-Gharbī
(or Burj Sikkat al-Qabr)
Burj Hārat az-Zammah ash-Sharqi
Burj Harat az-Zammah al-Gharbi
Masjid al-Fard
Masjid ash-Shaykh
Masjid ash-Shawādhinah
Burj Kharis Ballej
Burj al-Merzah
(Burj Bustān al-Qassam)
Bāb/Burj as-Sukhbi
Burj al-Methabhab

(Opposite page) Fig. 3: Plan of Harat Al ʿAqr settlement quarter, showing the location of gates and towers along the defensive wall, the four mosques within the quarter, and the location of Bait Al Saruj. The North Gate, Bab Al Hisn (or Bab Al Suq) and part of the north wall are no longer in existence. The plan also shows proposed projections of the town expansion and shift in defensive wall and *falaj* channel alignments over time (drawing: Briguglio, after base map in Consulting Engineering Services (CES) 2004, with additional information from Al Mahrooqi 2023). Gates: North Gate: Bab Al Hisn or (Bab Al Suq); East Gate: Bab Al Sabkhah; South Gate: Bab Abi al-Muthar; West gate: Bab Al Sukhbi (West Gate). Towers (clockwise from North Gate): Burj Al Ghawayr; Burj Al Khawarij; Burj Al Ballej; Burj Al Mahmoud; Burj Al ʿAliah; Burj Qataat Al Tawii; Burj Bustan Al ʿAqr Al Sharqi; Burj Bustan Al ʿAqr Al Gharbi (or Burj Sikkat Al Qabr); Burj Harat Al Zammah Al Sharqi; Burj Harat Al Zammah Al Gharbi; Burj Kharis Ballej; Burj Al Merzah (Burj Bustan Al Qassam); Burj Al Sukhbi (associated with West Gate); and Burj Al Methabhah.

the western gateway would have been the most elaborate, while the eastern, the smallest, was recently rebuilt. Another small eastern entrance has now entirely disappeared, replaced by vehicular access from the market.

The main street, over 300 m long, runs approximately north–south close to the eastern edge of the settlement and connects the northern entrance area to the southern gateway. An east–west oriented street of similar length extends from the western gateway to the main street. Another street of significant length runs parallel to the northern settlement wall. Several other streets and lanes complete the settlement structure and townscape. The western wall has the Falaj Dawt channel running along its interior between the towers (*burj*), Al Methabha and Kharis Ballej (Fig. 3).

Nizwa and heritage management in Oman

The development of conservation and heritage management policy took its first tentative steps with Oman joining UNESCO in 1972. This paralleled the processes of radical change and modernisation of the national socioeconomic and cultural infrastructure initiated as part of the Omani Renaissance (*nahḍa*). The National Heritage Protection Law (Royal Decree 6/1980), even though largely devoted to safeguarding archaeological sites and antiquities, was one of the earliest in the Arab region to explicitly state the need to protect built heritage. Conservation of built heritage, then understood as forts and castles, and religious structures of significance, focused on isolated monumental buildings often at the expense of adjoining traditional settlement quarters. Thus, the early restoration project undertaken by the Ministry of National Heritage and Culture in 1983 at Jabrin Castle, a mudbrick and stone construction, although a sympathetic restoration that interpreted well the various phases of construction, removed the quarter for the guards (*ʿaskarī*) to establish visitor parking.[4] Such interventions, as argued by Valeri (2009) and Benkari (2021), were symbolic and aimed at constructing a narrative about identity and a glorious past, depicting Oman as a unified country. Vernacular quarters were neglected and witnessed a progressive decay or unmanaged alteration of their original fabric, as no heritage management guidance was put in place (Benkari 2021).

Bahla Fort and Oasis World Heritage Site, however, marked an important transition. Since being added to the World Heritage Site list in 1987, various development projects that

4 Later the Ministry of Heritage and Culture (MHC), and now the Ministry of Heritage and Tourism (MHT) following Royal Decree 75/2020.

took place in the oasis threatened to compromise the integrity of the site. Thus, in 1998 the World Heritage Committee requested extending the original boundary of the protected area to include the oasis and highlighted the importance of developing a management plan to provide long-term guidance, tackling issues related to the conservation and preservation of the earthen constructions, as well as to provide solutions for the reuse of buildings that have lost their original integrity because of interventions employing construction practices unsuitable with the Outstanding Universal Values. Based on these recommendations, the Ministry commissioned the first oasis-wide heritage management plan (Atkins 2005). The plan relied on an extensive heritage audit but not comprehensive documentation, thus limiting the scope of analysis.

Planning in the early-1990s focused on the establishment of regional centres (Cowiconsult 1989; Cowiconsult 1991). In Nizwa – once the religious and intellectual centre of Ad Dakhiliyah – a new town centre was developed consisting of an entirely rebuilt market, a new Friday mosque and additional commercial premises, but it did not include the adjoining historically significant core, Harat Al ʿAqr or the wider oasis. The traditional settlement hierarchy which had developed over centuries was also altered in the process, and social networks disrupted. Subsequently, large-scale audits were undertaken and management plans developed for Al ʿAqr in the mid-2000s but never implemented (CES 2004). From the late-2000s the Ministry of Heritage and Tourism commissioned several heritage management plans for traditional settlement quarters through Omani and overseas academic institutions.[5] A very welcome initiative, these have nevertheless struggled to be realised except only partially at Misfat Al Abriyin; and the relentless alteration of urban and architectural fabric has continued, compromising heritage value in both public and private initiatives.

Since the government's commitment to promoting cultural tourism as one of the pillars of economic diversification, and the decision to privatise the management of heritage sites (TANFEEDH 2017), a local community- and investor-led process of rehabilitation of abandoned buildings has begun at pace, albeit without a specific framework in place (Benkari 2021). Nizwa and Al ʿAqr have become the focus of a growing interest in cultural tourism development, partly bolstered by its 2013 nomination as the Capital of Islamic Culture. Bawareq Nizwa International for Investment, a private developer company, has acquired several historic properties in Al ʿAqr for repurposing as guest houses and cafes (Benkari 2021; Al Riyami 2018). While this bottom-up initiative has provided much-needed tourism infrastructure, the focus has been on reproducing – mimicking – traditional aesthetics, and less on maintaining authenticity, historical significance, and crucially, typological and morphological characteristics. The agricultural land that once extended east–west through Al ʿAqr, for example, has been transformed into leisure and parking facilities, indelibly changing the settlement morphology.

Masjid Al Shawadhinah and the decorated *miḥrāb* tradition

Masjid Al Shawadhinah stands as an important reminder of the not-often-discussed artistic tradition that associated itself with the Ibadi revival in the fifteenth and sixteenth centuries. Also known as Masjid Al Qiblahtayn – a mosque with two *qibla* (direction of

5 These were awarded to: Sultan Qaboos, Nizwa and Buraimi universities, and the ArCHIAM research centre, then based at Nottingham Trent University, UK.

Fig. 4: Decorated prayer niche (*miḥrāb*) at Masjid Al Shawadhinah (a) and detail of Chinese porcelain inserts above the niche (b). Carved in gypsum, the decorated *miḥrāb* contains inscriptions and several translucent blue green glass roundels and five Chinese bowl and plate inserts, some of which are now missing or damaged. It was completed by the master craftsman, Isa bin Abdullah bin Yusuf of Bahla in May-June 1530 (Ramadan 936 AH) (photograph: Bandyopadhyay 2004).

prayer) – harking back to the early days of Islam when the Prophet decided to shift the direction of observance away from Jerusalem towards Mecca, it is one of only a handful of surviving Omani mosques retaining that special place in popular cultural memory. Sitting on a large (about 4 m high) plinth of compacted earth, the mosque is accessed via a staircase cut into the earthwork along its eastern edge, leading on to a large external prayer terrace (*ṣarḥ*) with an ablution facility (*wuḍū'*) on its southeastern corner. Typical of central-Omani Ibadi mosque organisation, the terrace provides lateral access to the prayer hall that occupies the entire northern part of the plinth (Costa 2001: 53–57). It is the decorated *miḥrāb*, however, that marks its special connection with the Ibadi revival and demands our attention, built towards the end of the imamate of Muhammad bin Ismail (c. 1500/01–1536). This beautiful example of gypsum carving, containing inscription and several translucent blue-green glass roundels and five Chinese bowl and plate inserts, was completed by the master craftsman (*naqqāsh*), Isa bin Abdullah bin Yusuf of Bahla in May–June 1530 (Ramadan 936 AH) (Fig. 4).[6] The inscription mentions the names of the patrons of the mosque, the master craftsperson, as well as the somewhat illegible name of the inscriber (Baldissera in Costa 2001: 242).

The Nabahina king (*malik*), Sulayman bin Sulayman bin Mudhaffar Al Nabhani, had heard an inner voice warning him that his rule – and his life – was to come to end soon. Hearing this, one of his chiefs advised the distraught Sulayman to retire to Nizwa, where his mind would be diverted from such worries by "what his heart desired and his eyes

6 The 26 glass inserts – a few missing, slightly varying in their hue and appearance, have a relatively wide rim and a shallow depression. The four small Chinese bowls surround the arch above the *miḥrāb* recess, and a shallow plate forms the central rosette. The survey was undertaken as part of the Arts and Humanities Research Council funded project, *Decorated Miḥrābs of Central Oman* (Bandyopadhyay 2003).

longed for" (Ibn Ruzayq 1871: 51). On the morning after his arrival Sulayman saw a woman and followed her to the wadi and was about to assault her when the woman fled to the nearby settlement quarter (*ḥāra*). Muhammad bin Ismail, a resident of Nizwa, responded to the woman's appeal for help, and in the confrontation that ensued, managed to kill Sulayman with his dagger. Sulayman may not have been slain; Ibn Ruzayq's above account differs slightly from Al Izkawi's narration which he closely follows, in which Sulayman is merely held down by Muhammad until the woman escapes and is later released (Al Izkawi 1874: 34). Nevertheless, Muhammad bin Ismail's bravery made the Nizwans rally behind him, and elect him the imam shortly afterwards (1500–01, 906 AH). Three years later (c. 1503–04), Sulayman and the Nabahina were finally defeated by the imamate forces, and their property confiscated, along with their Bani Ruwaha supporters.

This was not the first time that Nabahina property was confiscated by the resurgent Ibadi imamate. The previous instance was during the imamate of Umar bin Al Khattab, following Sulayman bin Sulayman's defeat at Hamamat at the hand of the Ibadi forces. A decree, confirmed in mid-August 1482 (887 AH), spearheaded by the chief qadi, ordered that Sulayman's property be confiscated and restored to those who had lost their possessions to unlawful usurpation. However, many remained "unknown, and their claims forgotten, and it was impossible in such cases to distribute the shares. All such unclaimed shares of the property were ordered to be given to the poor, and to expend it for the glory and maintenance of the government of the Musalmáns". Thus, where the claimants were unable to substantiate their claims, "that portion of the claim [came] under the head of unknown claims, and ... assigned to the poor, and taken charge of by the Imám" (Al Izqawi 1874: 32–33; also, Wilkinson 1987: 214).

"Thanks to this wealth", as Wilkinson mentions, "the new Imamate was able to survive in financial independence" (Wilkinson 1987: 215). The expenditure for the "glory ... of the government of the Musalmáns", it would seem, extended beyond establishing endowment (*waqf*) landholdings, to the rebuilding of mosques and the enthusiastic revival of the decorated *miḥrāb* tradition, following a hiatus of 250 years after the first one was built in 1252 at Saal.[7] A spirit of collaboration prevailed between the imamate government and the communities, as well as between shaykhly families across major oasis centres such as Nizwa, Bahla and Manah, undoubtedly underpinned by existing tribal political ties. Shaykh Wahab bin Ahmad and his son, Abdullah bin Wahab, patrons of the two earliest *maḥārīb* built in quick succession in Harat Al Bilad, Manah – at Masjid Al 'Ali (1504) and Masjid Al 'Ayn (1505), also very possibly supported the erection of the Masjid Al Jami' *miḥrāb* in Bahla (1511). The Wurud tribe (*nisba Al Wardi*), in particular, had had strong representations in both Manah and Bahla (Carter 1982: 125–126; Bandyopadhyay 2011: 133, 141–142). Abdullah bin Qasim bin Muhammad Al Humaymi, and Mushmil bin 'Umar bin Muhammad along with his son and grandsons, had built up a notable school of *miḥrāb* artisans in Manah, and worked across the three oasis towns and beyond, while Isa bin Abdullah bin Yusuf from Bahla created both the *maḥārīb* at Al Shawadhinah in Al 'Aqr, Nizwa and Al Jami' in Manah. The Al Shawadhinah *miḥrāb* records patrons that included the Bani Awf and the Abi Said (Umbu Said) tribes (Baldissera in Costa 2001: 242). The latter, an ancient tribe from Nizwa and leaders in Al 'Aqr, had strong familial connections with Bahla tribes, and

7 This is of course assuming that no *maḥārīb* were lost from the intervening period until the one completed at Masjid Al 'Ali in Harat Al Bilad, Manah on January 10, 1504 following the second confiscation, and during the early years of Muhammad bin Ismail's imamate.

had continued to play an important role in Harat Al ʿAqr (Wilkinson 1987: 125–126).[8] This strong Nizwa–Bahla connection may have further supported Isa bin Abdullah bin Yusuf's selection as the *miḥrāb* artisan for Shawadhinah.

Thus, by the mid-sixteenth century, Al Shawadhinah – its great antiquity reconfirmed and celebrated through the decorated *miḥrāb* – stood amidst episodes of strong cross-oasis community collaboration leading to repeated attempts at Ibadi resurgence. Collaboration also extended to the Indian Ocean ports on which Ad Dakhiliyah depended for trade and maritime access: to the Hormuzi port of Qalhat and the smaller independent port operations such as Qurayyat – the probable early sources of Chinese blue-and-white pottery into Ad Dakhiliyah. Sulayman bin Sulayman's grandfather, Mudhaffar bin Sulayman, hailed from the hinterland of Qurayyat, a Nabahina stronghold, and enjoyed excellent trading relationships with the ruler at Qalhat, Turanshah II. The latter had sought help of Omani – possibly Nabahina – merchants during the civil war with Saif Al Din, promising "repayment, gifts and customs exemptions". The capture of a richly-laden Chinese vessel on that occasion provided Turanshah II with the necessary resources. Sulayman bin Sulayman had married off his daughter to Salghur Shah, Turanshah's successor (Bhacker – Bhacker 2004: 38, 53; also, Wilkinson 1987: 214–215). The Chinese porcelain may well have turned up as dowry in the wealth confiscated from Sulayman and subsequently employed in the *miḥrāb*.[9]

Equally, Al Shawadhinah was witness to periodic destruction inflicted by external attacks or internal strife. And, both shaped urban form in Harat Al ʿAqr. In the interregnum that followed the killing of the first Ibadi imam, Al Julanda bin Masud (748–750), Nizwa was attacked by the Bani Muhariba (*nisba* Al Maharib) tribe in 762 (145 AH), and many of the allied Bani Nafiʿ and Bani Hamim tribes were either killed or fled Lower Nizwa (Al Izkawi 1874: 13–14; Ibn Ruzayq 1871: 9).[10] Following this attack Al ʿAqr was fortified during the imamate of the second Ibadi leader, Muhammad bin Abu Affan (793–795, 177–179 AH) (Al Mahrooqi 2024, personal communication). The civil strife that ensued from the late-nineth century onwards, which resulted in significant destruction of life and property across several oasis settlements, and at least two short-term occupations of Nizwa by governors appointed by the Caliphate, would have resulted in destruction but also further fortification attempts at Al ʿAqr (Al Izkawi 1874: 21–23).

Account of a second attempt at fortifying Al ʿAqr is recorded following two external attacks during Nabahina rule, possibly the earliest effort to enclose both settlement and agricultural land. The first attack was by the so-called Shirazi force which occupied Al ʿAqr

---

8 Badger, in his commentary on Ibn Ruzayq's history mistakenly identifies them (Benu Abi Sa'id) with the Al Bu Said tribe of Adam (Al Izkawi 1871: xxiii n. 1, 56; Banu Bu Said in Bathurst 1967: 56, 59). This is probably the case with Carter when he mentions that the Al Bu Said were prominent in Al ʿAqr in the days of the Ya'ariba Imam, Nasir bin Murshid (Carter 1982: 150). A later Umbu Said *ʿālim* from Al ʿAqr, Habib bin Salim Al Umbu Saidi Al ʿAqri Al Nizwani, supported Ahmed bin Said's election as imam.

9 Chinese porcelain found at sites in central Oman are mass-produced plates and bowls originating from the main industrial centres in southeast China (Goffriller *et al.* 2015). These may have arrived in Oman via India or East Africa with the dhow trade plying between secondary ports in the Western Indian Ocean region. Portuguese documents from 1507 relating to Muscat and Oman appear to have no mention of the import of porcelain goods (Al Salimi – Jansen 2015). The *maḥārīb* porcelain examples, on the other hand, bear strong similarity with objects retrieved from the late-fifteenth century Lena Shoal Junk wreck off the coast of the Philippines (Bandyopadhyay 2011: 265–270; Goddio *et al.* 2002).

10 The Bani Nafiʿ, resident in Al ʿAqr, were the direct forebears of both the Umbu Said of Al ʿAqr and the Mushaqisa (*nisba* Al Shaqsi) of Bahla via the Bani Ziyad lineage (Wilkinson 1977: 246; Wilkinson 1987: 125–126), while the Bani Hamim were the residents of Saal.

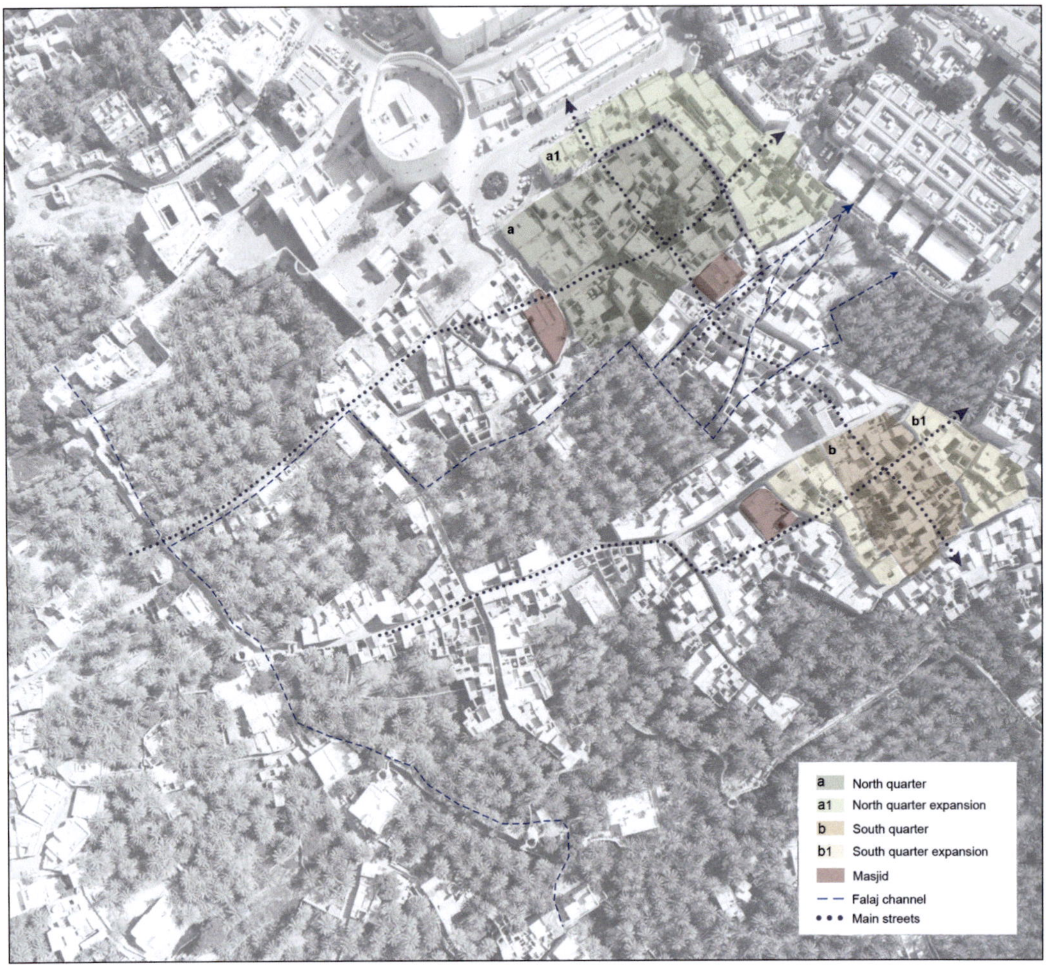

Fig. 5: Proposed projection of the expansion of the two core settlement quarters – North and South at Harat Al ʿAqr, and changes in its main pathways and *falaj* channel alignment resulting from the settlement quarter expansions (drawing: Briguglio, after aerial photo courtesy, National Survey Authority, Oman, for CES 2004).

for possibly about four months in either 1265–1266 (664 AH) or 1275–1276 (674 AH) and "ejected the principal persons ... from their houses", and took possession of properties (Al Izkawi 1874: 31–32; Ibn Ruzayq 1871: 36–40).[11] The other was the Awlad Ra'is attack in 1276 (675 AH) which surprised both the Nabahina *malik* and the people of Al ʿAqr. The Awlad Ra'is entered Al ʿAqr and created havoc in the space of half a day; they burned its *sūq* and places of commerce, and many lives were lost. "They plundered the place of all it contained, carried off the women, burned the magazines and the principal mosque. The books were likewise burned" (Al Izkawi 1874: 32).[12]

11 This occupation may have also coincided with an extensive famine which had a detrimental impact.

12 This is when the Friday Mosque at Saal took on a fortified appearance with the addition of a unique minaret in the form of a watch tower, which followed the erection of the first known Omani decorated *miḥrāb* there in 1252 (Bandyopadhyay 2011: 249–250).

The two core settlement quarters

From the early-Islamic period the existence of two core settlements could be identified and was certainly present at the time when this second fortification was erected (Fig. 5). It followed a pattern of nucleated settlement quarters that could be still seen in the wider Nizwa oasis, interlinked by pathways and *falaj* irrigation channels extending through the agricultural land (*cf.* Gaube – Gangler 2012: 222, 242–245). One, the North Quarter, was located immediately south of the fort constructed by Imam Al Salt bin Malik Al Kharusi (851–886/237–273 AH) with the intention to move the seat of the imamate away from the imam's own tribal base, and nearer to a large settlement quarter of a mixed tribal population (Wilkinson 1987: 79, 207). This quarter may have evolved from a more ancient and much smaller settlement cluster at the northern end of Harat Al ʿAqr. The other, the South Quarter, to the east of Masjid Al Shawadhinah, was separated from the North Quarter by a date palm plantation extending east as far as the wadi. The two quarters developed around the four ancient mosques: the first, Al Shawadhinah, reputedly built in 7 AH (628–629), the second, Al Shaykh, bearing the name of the noted early Ibadi *ʿālim*, Bashir bin Al Mundhir (eighth century), the third, Al Fard, reputedly built during the eleventh century, and the fourth, Al Muzaraʿah/Al Mazraʿah.[13]

While all Ibadi mosques have a raised plinth to distinguish the sacred domain from the dwellings and commercial buildings in a settlement quarter, Al Shawadhinah and Al Shaykh are particularly distinctive because of their very high compacted earth platforms. Their reputed antiquity but also typological similarity with field mosques around Al ʿAqr – such as the remains of the now disused Masjid Al Bayadir outside the western wall – would suggest its early beginnings on the edge of agricultural land (Fig. 6). Aside from giving prominence, the high plinth built with earth periodically excavated from the agricultural land was to protect the mosque from irrigation-induced water damage and the impact of various agricultural practices.[14] The epithet often used for Al Shawadhinah, Masjid Ra's Al ʿAqr, suggesting "a headland" or "a tip" or "the head" in addition to the great prestige, may further allude to its original prominence straddling the boundary between settlement quarter and agricultural land. The other mosque that is substantially raised from the street is Al Muzaraʿah/Al Mazraʿah; located further southeast of Al Shawadhinah, its name evidently refers to its position adjoining cultivated land. Masjid Al Fard does not have a significantly elevated plinth at present; however, as we argue below, at the time of its construction in the eleventh century, and even later, it would have stood on the edge of date palm gardens. The last vestiges of this garden, Mazraʿat Al Bustan, now converted to an extension of the *sūq* inside the wall, retains a drop of about 4 m from the main north–south street (Fig. 7).

Al Shaykh and Al Shawadhinah mosques originally stood outside the western edges of the two independent core settlements – the North and the South quarters – both located along the western bank of Wadi Kalbu. Al Fard, possibly slightly later in origin, and Al Muzaraʿah, stood on their southern edges. These settlements were fortified and re-fortified over several phases of expansion and consolidation, and the

---

13 Bashir bin Al Mundhir Al Nizwani was very likely one of the eight "carriers of knowledge" (*ḥamalat al-ʿilm*) who came to Oman from Basra (Al Rawas 2000: 209); there is also a possibility that this was his homonymous grandson from the mid-ninth century (Wilkinson 1987: 209).

14 This was also often the case with mosques located on the edge of wadis, where substantial retaining structures were employed (e.g., Costa 2001: 84–85; Bandyopadhyay 2011: 213–217).

Fig. 6: The remains of Masjid Al Bayadir outside the western wall is an example of field mosques raised on very high plinth and located on the edge of agricultural land (photograph: ArCHIAM, 2022).

Fig. 7: View of the now removed ruins of Bait Al Bustan from the garden, Mazra'at Al Bustan, across the main north-south street. The garden was the remains of a much more extensive agricultural presence within Al 'Aqr. The garden has now converted to an extension of the *sūq* inside the wall but retains a drop of about 4 m from the main street (photograph: Bandyopadhyay, 1993).

Fig. 8: Nizwa Fort, view from the wadi of the great round tower added during the time of Imam Sulṭan bin Sayf I al-Ya'rubi in the second half of the seventeenth century (photograph: ArCHIAM archive, courtesy, John Warr, 1972).

incorporation of the mosques would have been one of the earliest phases. This parallels examples of later settlement expansion and fortification at Harat Al Saybani in Birkat Al Mawz (Bandyopadhyay – Mershen 2022: 27–31), and at Harat Al Barashid in Sinaw (Bandyopadhyay *et al.* 2016). The two quarters were separated by date palm gardens which until the early-1970s extended as far as the wadi along an eastward sloping depression, possibly originally a minor wadi. It was irrigated by a distributary channel of Falaj Dawt that ran east–west through the garden.

The early-Islamic North Quarter would have had four entrances (Fig. 5). The northern access was likely to have been located across the wadi from the old Friday Mosque, east of the current access to the settlement. In the absence of the fort, which was only constructed during the imamate of Al Salt bin Malik Al Kharusi in the ninth century, the focus was on the ancient mosque built on a natural eminence of an isolated rock formation within the flood plain (Fig. 8 and Fig. 9). The route through the settlement thereafter followed a more cardinal north–south path, exiting through a southern gateway located west of Bait Al Saruj and Masjid Al Fard. A path through the agricultural land also arrived at the western entrance flanked by Masjid Al Shaykh, and extended towards the eastern gate, and to the wadi through further gardens lying beyond. The southward expansion of the North Quarter, which happened in at least three phases, gradually encroached on the gardens separating the North and South quarters and resulted in the redirection of the *falaj* channel on more than one occasion. The *falaj* channel watering this intervening garden flowed eastwards along its northern edge, and as its alignment suggests, would have pre-existed Masjid Al Fard. With each subsequent extension of the northern quarter, it either ran on the inside or skirted

Fig. 9: Aerial view of the original entrance square at Harat Al 'Aqr, defined by the imposing presence of the great round tower of Nizwa Fort. The access to the square is through the wide passage and a gate from the east, flanked on the north and east by the market buildings (photograph: courtesy, Henry Rogers, 1960).

around the outside of the newly established boundary/fortification. The first of these southward expansions that incorporated Masjid Al Fard – and thus, likely post-eleventh century, in the aftermath of the civil strife – ran through the present location of Bait Al Saruj and brought the *falaj* channel into the walled quarter.

This was followed by another expansion that shifted the boundary to the southern edge of the Bait, the passage of the *falaj* now directed first northeast towards the older channel, and later east. By this time a larger wall encompassing the entirety of Al 'Aqr had been built by the community in collaboration with the Nabahina kings following the devastating thirteenth century attacks. The need, therefore, for protecting the North Quarter would have significantly diminished, and the wall was now largely replaced by a passage. The abrupt truncation of the eastern city wall sentry-walk with a narrow opening next to the tower, Burj Al Ballej, and the position of the *sabla* (Sablat Al Kawarij), would suggest the passage of a pre-existing ancient channel out through the wall. A third expansion pushed the *falaj* to the final alignment that existed until the early-2000s. The last two southward expansion phases and changes in the pathway and *falaj* channel alignments, as we will discuss below, began during the Ya'ariba imamate and was completed in the Al Bu Said era. The eastward expansion may have taken place in two phases, eventually reaching the current configuration, possibly before the wall was finally restored and rebuilt and the present configuration established during the period of the Ya'ariba imam, Sultan bin Sayf I (1649–1680). The northern expansion would have taken place later, and although a small cluster of houses may have existed west of Al Shaykh Mosque, the area really developed following the arrival of the Al Bu Said and the erection of the encompassing city wall.

The South Quarter also went through several phases of development, many of which are still identifiable, although it is more difficult to ascertain the previous routes through the quarter. An earlier pathway beyond the North Quarter traversing across the garden would have passed through the settlement quarter. A wide, open space originally separated Masjid Al Shawadhinah from the western edge of this compact quarter, with a gate providing passage through it to the eastern gardens. The original western fortification alignment is still identifiable as it now forms the edge of a passage that runs north to south. To this, two phases of expansion were added, which encroached on the open space, eventually leaving only a narrow lane between the mosque and the western boundary. A further expansion took place south of Al Shawadhinah mosque, possibly establishing a new fortified western boundary and a southwest gate. Another passage – this, the remnants of the earlier eastern boundary – separates the extension on the east. Further expansions took place along the southern boundary and the southeast.

The Ya'ariba imamate, the city wall and new urbanism

The brief period of stability and calm promised during the early years of Muhammad bin Ismail's imamate began to fall apart towards the end of his life (d. April/May 1536), a dispute that spilled over into the imamate of his successor, his son Barakat bin Muhammad (1535–1565?), when rival imams were installed in both Nizwa and Manah.[15] The instability allowed a Nabahina revival, and one of their rulers, *malik* Sultan bin Muhsin bin Sulayman bin Nabhan, was able to capture Nizwa in 1557 (Al Izkawi 1874: 34; Wilkinson 1987: 216). The Ibadi quest for the ideal spiritual leader (imam) who would also provide strong temporal leadership continued through the latter part of the sixteenth century. And so did the struggle for gaining control over key settlements of Ad Dakhiliyah among the many *mulūk*, more concerned about narrow personal gains, using tribal warfare and oppressive means to secure control. Under these circumstances in 1624 Nasir bin Murshid was elected imam by the *'ulamā'* community headed by the influential *'ālim*, Khamis bin Said Al Shaqsi from the Bahla Mushaqisa shaykhly lineage (Al Izkawi 1974: 46–47; Wilkinson 1987: 126). As always, Al 'Aqr and Nizwa became the centre of the struggle to establish the new Ya'ariba imamate. After an initial failed attempt to capture Nizwa from the north, which Nasir had decided to abort after receiving "no confirmation of support from the garrison of the Fort" (Bathurst 1967: 57), he was successful the second time approaching Al 'Aqr from Izki in the south, and was welcomed by the residents.

However, while in Al 'Aqr, Nasir was made aware in advance of a rebellion from the prominent Bani Bu Said (Umbu Said) family resident there, and managed to eject them without any major confrontation (Bathurst 1967: 58–59), which must have been only partial and temporary. To Nasir's annoyance, the Umbu Said were received by Sayf bin Muhammad Al Hina'i in Bahla, possibly on the basis of their strong familial connections there, and Nasir's temporary ally, Mani' bin Sinan Al 'Umayri in Samail. Shortly afterwards Sayf bin

15 This was mainly due to his failure, as the leading *qadi* from Al 'Aqr, Ahmad bin Maddad critically pointed out, to condemn or rescind the potentially unlawful original confiscation of properties of two individuals in 1482, and his increasingly oppressive behaviour of forcibly imposing unjust taxation on his subjects without providing "protection and security" (Al Izkawi 1874: 34–35; Wilkinson 1987: 346 n. 23). During the imamate of his successor, his son Barakat bin Muhammad (1535–1565?), the same Al 'Aqr *qadi* and his followers set up a rival imam, Umar bin Al Qasim Al Fudayli, and yet another, Abdullah bin Muhammad Al Qurn was elected by the people of Manah in 1560 (Al Izkawi 1874: 34; Wilkinson, 1987: 216).

Fig. 10: View east of the wide passage between the main entrance square and the market at Harat Al ʿAqr. The tower, Burj Al Ghawayr, is visible on the right (photograph: courtesy, Henry Rogers, 1960).

Muhammad and Maniʿ bin Sinan raised a force, returned and took over Al ʿAqr with the secret assistance of some of the resident tribes, and besieged the imam in the fort. The situation was saved when reinforcements arrived from Izki and Bahla that included the imam's steadfast supporters, the Bani Riyam, and many from the besieging forces were slain (Al Izkawi 1874: 49–50; Bathurst 1967: 77).

The scare caused by the potential Umbu Said rebellion or the siege that actually materialised, or both, prompted Nasir bin Murshid to rebuild and strengthen the ninth century fort at Al ʿAqr in the mid/late-1620s. A key consideration would have been – in the Omani context – the shift to hybrid warfare incorporating the widespread use of firearms. The imposing round tower was added during the time of his successor, Imam Sultan bin Sayf I, reputedly financed from the wealth acquired through the Omani attack on the Portuguese port of Diu on the Indian coast (Bathurst 1967: 137; Wilkinson 1987: 181). This tower, approximately circular in plan of about 43 m in diameter and a height of 30 m, reputedly took 12 years to build. If this unique commission was entirely financed by the spoils of Diu, then the work would have begun at the earliest in early 1669, after the first attack on Diu in November–December 1668 (Bathurst 1967: iv, 135) and completed in 1681, at least a year after his death. However, this timeline does not align with other suggested dates, such as 1660 (d'Errico 1983: 303) or 1668. It is probable that the work began earlier and was supported subsequently by the spoils from Diu and several other conquests across the Western Indian Ocean region, resulting in a gradual consolidation of the Ya'ariba maritime empire. A unique tower unmatched in the entirety of the Arabian Peninsula, its role was to "provide a dominant position to control the oasis and the surrounding routes from the Wadi Samail and the more remote desert regions" (d'Errico 1983: 303). Yet another example of the penetration of maritime trade and overseas influence, it was also to inspire awe through its distinctive and unprecedented form, proportion and towering prominence.

With the fort and the round tower in place, a new north entrance to Harat Al ʿAqr was established (Fig. 10). A large square was formed facing the fort entrance, entered through a formidable archway on the east, with a *sabla* along its northern edge for the formal reception of dignitaries and holding meetings. The new fort entrance and wall was now aligned with the ancient western boundary of the North Quarter of Harat Al ʿAqr, which, with the fall of the original core settlement walls, had transformed into a passageway oriented north–south, connected with part of the original west–east passage. The impact of the significant destruction wrought by the two Persian attacks in the thirteenth century, and the turmoil between the mid-1550s and late-1620s, would have resulted in a substantial loss in building stock, especially in the North Quarter, leaving major gaps in the built fabric. Over the next century these were gradually filled in with interventions producing a new alignment of the original north–south route, and the gradual settling of new arrivals within agricultural land.

With the return of stability and the movement of tribal groups encouraged by opportunities the new Ibadi imamate provided, rebuilding the quarters became a priority. Sultan bin Sayf I also invested in the rebuilding and restoration of the Al ʿAqr city wall, supported by the expanding wealth of the imamate from maritime trade, overseas acquisitions, some taxation, agricultural reform and from "residue of estates for which there are no entitled heirs ... which reverts to the state" (Wilkinson 1987: 180–183; also, Bandyopadhyay – Mershen 2022: 22–25 on agricultural land development). While the exact extent of the city wall rebuilding cannot be established, there are sections where sentry-walks and turrets were added to build a more formidable and defendable fortification system and a cohesive urban identity. Originally freestanding, these modifications could be seen along substantial sections around the northwestern corner but also the eastern and southern city walls.

This final wall configuration was to a large extent defined by the need to protect *waqf* land and property acquired during the early-sixteenth century, and continued to be maintained, at least partially, by endowment allocations. Once walled in, the land east of Masjid Al Muzaraʿah was severed from its original water supply, which now fell outside the quarter, and thus needed a new agricultural well that employed cattle for drawing water (*zājrah*/*zaygrah*). However, the area was also subject to further encroachment that gradually reduced the arable land. The decision to incorporate the *falaj* channel along the western wall required maintaining water negotiations with communities outside the wall; thus, a shared *falaj* inspection arrangement was created by setting back Burj Al Madhbagah on the northwestern corner. Later, in the early-twentieth century, new civic developments straddled this section of the channel; a new *sabla* was built along the western wall at the southern end of a small cluster of houses, and a women's prayer area (*majāza*) emerged slightly east of it.

This very formidable defence arrangement may provide a clue about the earlier wall configuration, which, as we know, took place following the two successive and devastating Persian attacks during the Nabahina period. A city wall of a more irregular configuration had emerged at that time and possibly without sentry walks, itself a result of several previous expansion, consolidation and rebuilding phases. For a period the city wall may have coexisted with older fortifications for the North and South settlement

Fig. 11: Partial view of Ḥarat Al `Aqr looking south, showing the location of Bait Al Saruj off the main street on the left. The four ancient mosques that characterise the settlement quarter are also visible: Masjid Al Shaykh is in the right foreground; Masjid Al Fard is partially visible along the left frame; Masjid Al Shawadhinah, the largest of the Al 'Aqr mosques is visible in the middle-right of the image; and Masjid Al Muzara'ah is located at the farthest end of the settlement (photograph: courtesy, Henry Rogers, 1960).

quarters.[16] In Nizwa, at least two previous city wall configurations could be proposed (see Fig. 3). The first ran roughly parallel to the current eastern boundary through Burj Al Ballej as far as Burj Al ʿAliya, then followed the southern boundary of the South Quarter to Masjid Al Shawadhinah, where it cut back to a longer stretch of the southern wall, its path still indicated by the "dog-legged" configuration of two pathways. The western wall ran along the present north–south pathway as far north as the current southern edge of the fort where it connected with the northern boundary. Further westward expansion formed at least another free-standing wall running north–south, possibly connecting with Burj Merzah (Burj Bustan Al Qassam) and by then a more irregularly evolving southern wall.

Bait Al Saruj and the timber crafting tradition

The recently refurbished Bait Al Saruj stands at the intersection of several morphological phases of Harat Al ʿAqr but also as an important reminder of the penetration into Ad Dakhiliyah of a mid-eighteenth century artistic tradition that had its roots in Oman's long maritime association. Owned by a prominent Al Bu Said family, this distinctively configured three-storied building – a product of its particular location and lateral access – deviates from the usual frontally accessed deep spatial organisation of Nizwan houses (Fig. 12). The

16 This is similar to what is still evident at Harat Al ʿAqr in Bahla, where expanding and gradually coalescing settlement cores needed new fortifications and entrances (e.g., gateways Hawashim and Nargila) which coexisted with older ones (Bandyopadhyay *et al.* 2014).

Fig. 12: Bait Al Saruj in Al ʿAqr, partial view of eastern façade showing the first floor reception hall (a, photograph: Bandyopadhyay, 2004) and ground floor plan (b, drawing: Briguglio, after drawing in CES, 2004).

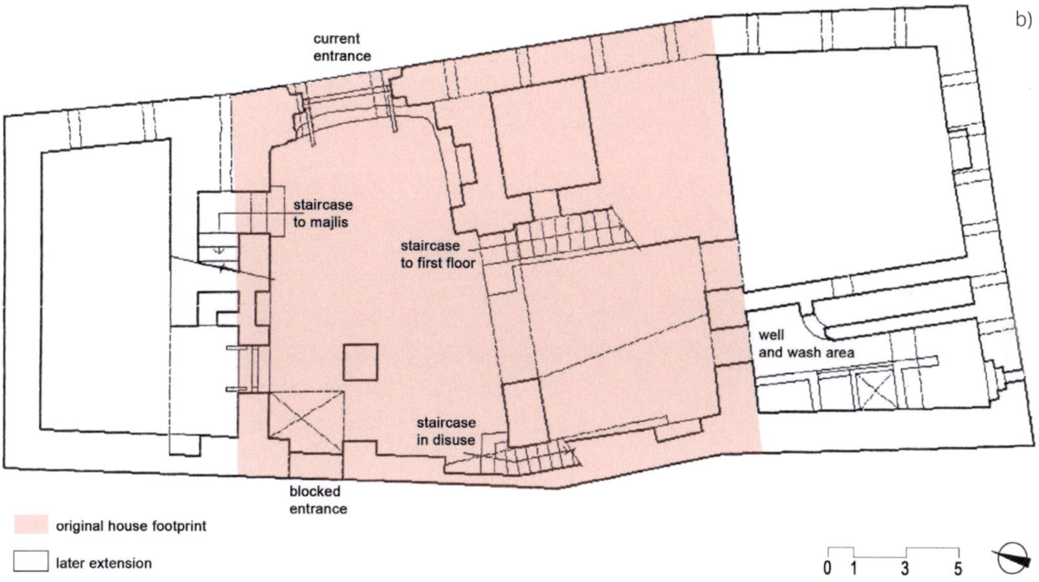

ground floor consists of four bays that span the entirety of the narrow, elongated plan. The access door is on the east façade, from the main path that runs between the north and the south gates. The deep double wall on the ground floor separates the northernmost bay from the entrance area. Almost certainly tracing the original alignment of the wall that encircled the North Quarter but perhaps even a remnant of that, it later provided support for a staircase giving direct access to the first-floor reception hall.

The main staircase to the upper floors is at right angles and to the left of the entrance, leaving it hidden following the principles of organisation that offered maximum privacy to its residents. However, unusually, another disused staircase, partly built into the western wall, was flanked by a blocked entrance, which directly faced the present entrance. An original access through this western entrance could only have provided the necessary privacy to justify this staircase placement. Although another building now adjoins this western wall, an older pathway alignment could be read along this façade, once connecting with an original northern entrance into the South Quarter. Thus, Bait Al Saruj would have been built – possibly as a smaller and humble, single-floor dwelling – with an original entrance on the west at a time when this western pathway was still functioning, and at least parts of the older North Quarter wall was in situ.

Bait Al Saruj changed to an eastern entrance as the emphasis gradually shifted to the current pathway alignment. This would have happened during the late-Ya'ariba period or early Al Bu Said era, as the existing single-storied property was very likely bought over by the Al Bu Said family, expanded and completed in the 1740s. The southern end of the ground floor – originally absent – was added to complete the building footprint; the shift in the building's orientation at this end resulted from its alignment with the pre-existing pathway and redirected *falaj* channel that now flowed slightly northeast into the older channel towards the eastern gardens. The building adjoining Bait Al Saruj to the west was possibly constructed in two phases, as the old western pathway lost its importance and shifted alignment westwards. The pathway reorganisations resulted in an evolved, much deeper, land configuration south of Bait Al Saruj, evident in houses such as Bait Al Bustan, which extended westwards on at least three occasions.

It is one of the rooms facing the second-floor terrace that provides a clear understanding of the building's *terminus ad quem*, and a fascinating story of maritime cultural transference across Oman. There, the roof beams were supported by beautifully designed timber brackets with a distinctive two-pronged motif on their soffits cupping between them a bulbous protrusion. Interestingly, this motif is also found on beam supports at one of the prominent Al Bu Said houses at Harat Al Bilad in Manah. In the walled quarter of Al Bilad, the Al Bu Said developed their houses on agricultural land as the tribe expanded their tribal base (*dār*) north from the Adam oasis in the eighteenth century. In Manah the brackets were decorated with an additional band of diamond-shaped motifs at their base. A more elaborate and polychrome version was present at the fortified house, Al Qasr (or Al Fath) Al Bu Said in Bawshar near Muscat, and this is where the clue to their origin lies (Fig. 13).

In Bawshar the Al Bu Said diaspora had established yet another base. The settlements of Al Fath and Sad – or Fathayn (two or joint victories or conquests), a term often used to collectively refer to the twin quarters – was not just the summer retreat for the governor (*wali*) of Muscat but provided a secure political and defensive base for the newly founded Al Bu Said imamate. The two settlement quarters were established early in the Al Bu Said era, possibly by 1748 CE (c. 1160 AH, Al Bu Saidi 2016: 92), soon after Imam Ahmad bin Said's accession to power following the overthrow of the last Ya'arubi ruler, Sayf bin Sultan II in early 1740s. These new quarters were built away from the older and well-established areas of Bawshar.

The Qasr Al Bu Said at Al Fath, an early Al Bu Said effort in creating monumental architecture, was a substantial fortified dwelling, square in plan with towers at diagonally opposite corners. It followed the Ya'ariba approach to the design of castles and fortified buildings at locations such as Jabrin and Al Hazm. In emulating the Ya'ariba castles – architectural forms so deeply ingrained in the Omani mind as representations of stability

Fig. 13: Timber beam supports from Bait Al Saruj in Harat Al ʿAqr, Nizwa (a); Bait Al Kabir in Harat Al Bilad, Manah (b); and Qasr (or Al Fath) Al Bu Said in Al Fath, Bawshar (c) (photographs: Bandyopadhyay, 2010, 2004 & 1994).

and prosperity – the Al Bu Said at Bawshar were claiming their legitimate role at the temporal and spiritual helm. However, at least one architectural element – the distinctive two-pronged beam support design – appear to have come from a different direction. They do not appear to feature in Ya'ariba buildings; Jabrin castle, for example, has a Persianate foliate design for its beam supports (Fig. 14). They appear, on the other hand, to bear strong resemblance to examples from a distant Iberia. Thirteenth and fourteenth century painted timber ceiling designs in civil buildings from the Spanish regions of Conca de Barberà, lower Segarra and Ibiza show marked similarity in the design and decorative treatment of the bracket supports (Abárzuza *et al.* 2018; Fuguet Sans – Mirambell Abancó 2013; Fig. 15) Prominent vegetal, zoomorphic and humanoid motifs found carved and painted in the Iberian examples appear to have been somewhat simplified in the Omani examples.

Pending further research, this virtually implausible connection may have an explanation in the Portuguese occupation of Muscat. Fathayn was masterminded by Khamis bin Salim bin Muhammad bin Khalaf Al Bu Saidi, a cousin of Imam Ahmad bin Said. He was quick to identify the importance of Bawshar as a strategic retreat. Khamis bin Salim was born in c. 1708 (c. 1120 AH, Al Bu Saidi 2016: 36) in the Al Bu Said quarter of Harat Al Jamiʿ in Adam.[17] His astute political skills led him to work closely with Ahmad bin Said, and played an important role in the eviction of the invading Persians. Khamis directed the imamate army, and very skilfully addressed the property disputes that ensued in Muscat and Muttrah as the erstwhile inhabitants returned to towns destroyed by the invaders (Al Bu Sa'idi 2016: 36; also, Al Izkawi 1871: 152–154).

17 Having faced hardship in Adam in his early life, he had moved to Rustaq, where he was possibly in the employ of the Yaʿariba imam. During that time, apparently, he lived in Wibil (Wabal/Manal), married there and bought properties and acquired shares in two of the *aflāj* (Al Bu Sa'idi 2016: 42). I am grateful to my colleague, Ataa Alsalloum for helping with the translation of the text.

Fig. 14: Persianate foliate design for beam support in Jabrin castle (photograph: courtesy, Henry Rogers, 1960).

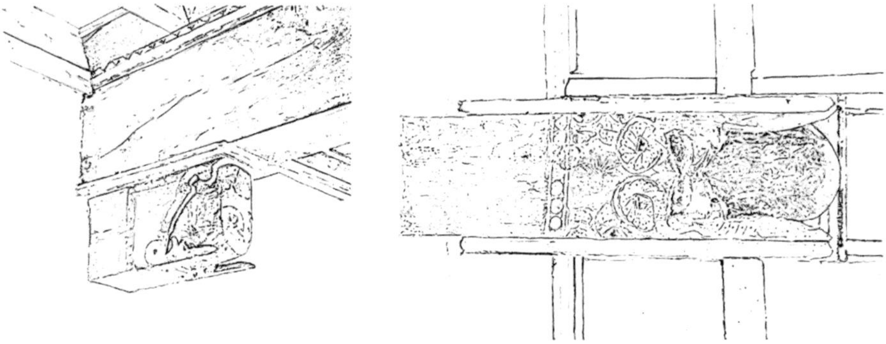

Fig. 15: Drawings of a timber beam support from the old town hall of Ibiza, now part of the Universitat d'Eivissa, Ibiza, Spain (drawing: Briguglio, after Abárzuza *et al.* 2018: 31, 35).

While all examples of Portuguese civil architecture in Muscat have now disappeared, the Augustinian monastery (later known as *Bait Al Gharayzah*) may have been the possible Iberian example wherefrom Khamis drew his inspiration. Khamis bin Salim, who was appointed the wali of Muscat very early during Imam Ahmed's rule, will have visited the monastery which provided the brief sojourn for Ya'ariba and Al Bu Said imams until Hamad bin Said bin Ahmad made the port town the de facto capital of Oman in the late-1780s. The crafting inspiration he possibly drew from the monastery was introduced into Al Fath, and later transferred to other prominent Al Bu Said properties across Oman via a consistent group of artisans.

Conclusion

This chapter discussed the close relationship between socially embedded artistic practices and the formation of resilient "urban artifacts" in traditional settlements, drawing on the example of Harat Al Aqr quarter in the Nizwa oasis of Oman. Enriched by evolved histories, distinctive forms and individuality of character, such artifacts act as fulcrums around which settlements develop, and thus they play an important role in characterising settlement morphology. We focused on three "artistic tradition–urban artifact" nexuses – decorative *miḥrāb* and Masjid Al Shawadhinah, city wall-building and the eighteenth century "new" urban form of Al ʿAqr, and timber crafting tradition and Bait Al Saruj – to illustrate their closely interactive nature and pivotal role in establishing Al ʿAqr as the centre of Nizwa. The decorated *miḥrāb* installation in the early-sixteenth century enhanced the character of the ancient Masjid Al Shawadhinah, which played a central role in shaping the form and identity of Al ʿAqr. The late-seventeenth-century city wall, a product of evolution over centuries, provided the final urban form and social cohesion. The mid-eighteenth century timber crafting tradition at Bait Al Saruj arguably signalled a morphological finality, *intra muros*. Consistently projecting and interpreting Ibadi politico-cultural ideals, and yet contrary to the perception of an isolated and introspective landlocked Ad Dakhiliyah region, our assessment shows a world perpetually attuned with Indian Ocean maritime trade and relationships.

This above discussion also highlights the importance of safeguarding both urban artifacts and morphology for urban heritage conservation, and thus underpinning all conservation initiatives with an approach based on sound morphological knowledge. Such knowledge is essentially collaborative, with communities and specialists intersecting; without this, many of the urban artifacts and morphological characteristics at Harat Al ʿAqr are under threat from the pace of tourism infrastructure development as heritage values and significances are progressively erased. The revised Cultural Heritage Law (Royal Decree, 35/2019, amended by 41/2020), while providing a more complete framework and governance structure for heritage conservation and management in Oman, continues to define cultural heritage assets as isolated structures and buildings independent of the fabric of the settlement. The Ministry of Heritage and Tourism remains the sole authority responsible for enlisting such assets on the Oman Cultural Heritage Register, preserving and managing heritage sites, and providing planning permissions for all civic redevelopments.[18] A devolved decision-making responsibility involving the local municipalities would help raise awareness of conservation and adaptive reuse considerations as distinct from conventional new build practices, and pave the way for robust regulatory framework development.

18 In the case of privately owned sites, the owner is responsible for their preservation and maintenance, while the Ministry should provide financial or in-kind support. However, the law also specifies that expropriation of abandoned buildings can be required for public benefit (RD35/2019; Khalil – Nasr 2021).

References

Abárzuza, A. F. – Serra, C. T. – Gonzálvez, J. J. 2018
Mirando Hacia Arriba: El Artesonado de la Casa de la Universitat, Sede del Museu Arqueològic de Dalt Vila (Ibiza, Islas Baleares), *Fites* 18, 26-43.

Al Bu Saidi, K. S. A. 2016
Ṭalā'iḥ al-fatḥ (The Pioneers of Conquest), a history of Bawshar, Al Fath and Sad (second edition), Muscat: Al Dhamri Library.

Al-Izkawi, Sirhán b. Sa'id b. Sirhán b. Muhammad (attributed; Ross, E.C. *tr.*). 1874
Annals of Oman (*kashf al-ghumma: al-jami' li akhbar al-umma*), Calcutta: Baptist Mission Press.

Al Mahrooqi, A. H. 2023
Harat al-'Aqr. [conference presentation, Challenges and Opportunities of Housing Rehabilitation in Historic Settlements, Morocco: UN-Habitat, December 2023].

Al Rawas, I. 2000
Oman in Early Islamic History, Reading: Ithaca Press.

Al Riyami, A. 2018
Nizwa old houses now turn into "Heritage Hotel", *Oman Observer* (June 26, 2018). https://www.omanobserver.om/article/53768/Head%20stories/nizwa-old-houses-now-turn-into-heritage-hotel [accessed 13.01.2025].

Al Salimi, A. – Jansen, M. 2015
Portugal in the Sea of Oman: Religion and Politics, Baden-Baden: Georg Olms Verlag.

Australia ICOMOS 2013
The Burra Charter: The Australia ICOMOS Charter for Places of Cultural Significance, Burwood (VIC): Australia ICOMOS Incorporated.

Bandyopadhyay, S. 2003
The Decorated Mihrabs of Central Oman. Research project funded by the Arts and Humanities Research Board, AHRB (now the Arts and Humanities Research Council, AHRC).

Bandyopadhyay, S. 2011
Manah: Omani oasis, Arabian legacy: architecture and social history of an Omani oasis settlement, Liverpool: Liverpool University Press.

Bandyopadhyay, S. – Goffriller, M. – Quattrone, G. – Harrison, J. – Reza, M.H. – Al Abri, H.N. 2014
Documentation and heritage management plan, Harat al-'Aqr, Bahla fort and oasis World Heritage site, Dakhiliyah Governorate, Muscat: Ministry of Heritage and Culture.

Bandyopadhyay, S. – Goffriller, M. – Quattrone, G. Reza, M.H. – Al Abri, H.N. 2016
Documentation and heritage management plan, Sinaw oasis, North Sharqiyyah Governorate [unpublished report, Muscat: Ministry of Heritage and Culture].

Bandyopadhyay, S. – Mershen, B. 2022
Falaj communities in Oman: A case for local governance? Ibadi legal rulings and spatial and ethnohistorical observations, *Journal of Material Cultures in the Muslim World* 3/1: 6-47. DOI:10.1163/26666286-12340028

Bathurst, R. B. 1967
The Ya'rubi dynasty of Oman [PhD thesis, University of Oxford].

Benkari, N. 2021
Community-led Initiatives for the rehabilitation and management of vernacular settlements in Oman: A phenomenon in the making, *Built Heritage* 5: 21. DOI:10.1186/s43238-021-00039-5

Bhacker M. R. – Bhacker B. 2004
Qalhat in Arabian history: Context and chronicles, *The Journal of Oman Studies* 13: 11-56.

Carter, J. R. L. 1982
Tribes of Oman, London: Routledge.

CES (Consulting Engineering Services) 2004
Harat al-'Aqr: Conservation and development project: Survey documentation and master plan [unpublished report, Muscat: Ministry of Regional Municipalities, Environment and Water Resources].

Costa, P. M. 2001
Historic mosques and shrines of Oman. British Archaeological Reports International Series 938. Oxford: Archaeopress.

Cowiconsult 1989
Nizwa town structure plan: Report of survey 1 [unpublished report. Muscat: Ministry of Housing].

Cowiconsult 1991
A'Dakhliya regional plan: Phase 3, Final report [unpublished report. Muscat: Ministry of Housing].

d'Errico, E. 1983
Introduction to the Omani military architecture of the sixteenth, seventeenth and eighteenth centuries, *The Journal of Oman Studies* 6/2: 291-306.

Figuet Sans, J. – Mirambell Abancó, M. 2013
Els Sostres Teginats Policroms dels Segles XIII i XIV a la Conca de Barberà i la Baixa Segarra, *Quaderns del MEV* (Museu Episcopal de Vic) 6: 119-137.

Gaube, H. – Gangler, A. 2012
Transformation processes in oasis settlements of Oman, Muscat.

Goddio, F. – Crick, M. – Lam, P. – Pierson, S. – Scott, R. 2002
Lost at sea: The strange route of the Lena Shoal junk, London: Periplus Publishing.

Goffriller, M. – Ma, H. – Bandyopadhyay, S. – Henderson, J. 2015.
Chinese porcelains and the decorations of Omani mihrabs, *Proceedings of the Seminar for Arabian Studies* 45: 123-138.

Ibn Ruzayq, Humayd bin Muhammad bin Ruzayq/ Raziq bin Bakhit al-Nakhli (Badger, E.C. *tr.*). 1871
History of the Imâms and Seyyids of Omân (*al-fath al-mubin fi sirat al-Busa'idiyin*), London: Hakluyt Society.

Khalil, M. A. M. – Nasr, E. H. M. 2021
The development of legal framework for the management of World Heritage Sites in Oman: A case study on Bahla oasis, *Journal of Cultural Heritage Management and Sustainable Development* 13/1: 146-166. DOI:10.1108/JCHMSD-07-2020-0106

Rossi, A. 1982.
Architecture of the City. Cambridge (Mass.) & London: MIT Press.

Royal Decree 6/1980
Promulgating the National Heritage Protection Law (February 10, 1980), Government of Oman. https://qanoon.om/p/1980/rd1980006/ (Arabic) [accessed 13.01.2025].

Royal Decree 35/2019
Promulgating the Cultural Heritage Law (May 2, 2019), Government of Oman. https://qanoon.om/p/2019/rd2019035/ (Arabic) [accessed 13.01.2025].

Royal Decree 41/2020
Amending some provisions of the Cultural Heritage Law (March 31, 2020), Government of Oman. https://decree.om/2020/rd20200041/ (Arabic) [accessed 13.01.2025].

Royal Decree 75/2020.
Regarding the Administrative Apparatus of the State (August 12, 2020). Government of Oman. https://qanoon.om/p/2020/rd2020075/ (Arabic) [accessed 10.02.2025].

Scholz 1978
Sultanate of Oman, Aerial Photographic Atlas: Natural regions and living areas in text and photographs II, Stuttgart: Ernst Klett.

TANFEEDH (The National Program for Enhancing Economic Diversification) 2017
Tanfeedh Handbook, Muscat: Government of Oman.

Valeri, M. 2009
Oman: Politics and society in the Qaboos state, London: Hurst & Company.

Wilkinson, J.C. 1977
Water and tribal settlement in south-east Arabia: A study of the aflaj of Oman, Oxford: Clarendon Press.

Wilkinson, J. C. 1987
The imamate tradition of Oman, Cambridge: Cambridge University Press.

W. S. Atkins 2005
Bahla Fort and Oasis World Heritage Site Management Plan [unpublished report, Muscat: Ministry of Heritage and Culture].

#Mudbrick #Oman

On the Tourist Perception of Abandoned *Ḥārāt* Architecture

Josephine Kanditt and Thomas Schmidt-Lux

Introduction[1]

March 2023. We are driving through Oman, a hundred kilometres west of Muscat. We are looking for the old settlement of Imti, which has been recommended to us as a particularly beautiful and artistic place. We drive through the village, which doesn't look very busy in the late afternoon. With one eye looking out of the car and the other on the smartphone and Google Maps, we navigate our way through the village. We almost miss the entrance of the old settlement, which is located on a bend; it's only with a second look that we notice the café, which points to a tourist attraction. We park on the side of the road and walk to the settlement. It is indeed special and worth a visit: a kind of main path leads through the old settlement structure, along which some of the facades have been renovated. There are cushions in many of the window openings, indicating that people stay there in the evenings when it gets cooler. The electricity pylons are colourfully painted and there are small drawings on the walls here and there. We are very touched and also surprised; we have never seen such loving use of the old settlements before.

Two things are interesting about this episode. Firstly, Imti is an example of the recently increasing efforts of local Omani initiatives to revive the formerly abandoned settlements. Examples of this can also be found in other places, such as Al Hamra and Birkat Al Mawz.[2] Imti is special in that it is not only investing in cafés and guest houses, but the revitalizations

1 We would like to thank Uta Karstein for her valuable advice, particularly on the sociological analysis of tourism, Leonie Biagioni for her many years of valuable work on the project, and Nana Kamkamidze for help with the translation.

2 Since the late 1990s and increasingly since the 2010s, revitalization measures can be observed in the village of Al Hamra. With the Bait Al Safa, a museum in the old settlement of the village, a contact point has been created alongside other renovated houses, which now house a number of small hotels, providing specific information about Omani (building) traditions and the way of life in the settlements. See also: https://www.omanobserver.om/article/1138265/features/travel/why-al-hamras-living-museum-bait-al-safah-continues-to-stand-today, last accessed on 28.02.2024.

in: S. Döpper – B. Mershen – J. Kanditt – I. Biezeveld – T. Schmidt-Lux (eds) 2025, *Mudbrick Settlements of the Oman Peninsula. Inhabited – Abandoned – Re(dis)covered*, Leiden: Sidestone Press, 119–132.

are in more of an artistic nature and reuse is also being carried out by the local population.[3] So it is also, but not only, tourists who are starting to find the former residential buildings attractive and are now putting them to new uses.

On the other hand, our lengthy search for the settlement is notable. Because for those of us unfamiliar with the area, it was by no means easy to find the settlement. There was no sign at the entrance to the village pointing to this place, nor were there any signs in the village itself. And the café wasn't advertised very prominently either. Again, we needed the help of Google to find our destination. In short, the old settlement in Imti was not immediately and easily visible. And even in the settlement itself, there were hardly any clues as to why these numerous houses were now empty, what had happened to them before and what they had been used for and by whom.

We had similar experiences not only in Imti. In many other places too, our local experts showed us the way to an old settlement, about which we had also learned from experts. In other cases, however, we knew about the settlements, had already read about them in travel guides or seen photos in blogs. Obviously, the settlements were all accessible and open to the public. However, the settlements were visible in the sense that they were pointed out (in whatever form) in different ways and to varying degrees.

Visibility, attention and the tourist gaze

Questions of visibility and invisibility are interesting from a sociological perspective, and have increasingly occupied the social sciences for some time. This is based on the assumption that the visibility of people or things is also linked to their position in social space. In other words, questions of visibility are closely linked to questions of power, social recognition, and relevance.

What exactly is meant by visibility is part of the debate. Some positions imply empirical, sensory accessibility, while others use the term more metaphorically (*cf.* Brighenti 2007). From an analytical point of view, the most productive positions are those that relate the two. Visibility then results from the interplay of empirical accessibility and questions of power. In the sociological sense, people and things are visible if they can be seen (whether directly or mediated by the media) and if this happens in important places or media.

Visibility, as the German sociologist Markus Schroer has pointed out, often goes hand in hand with attention; the two are closely related. "The contemporary discourse on visual culture indicates a privileging of the visible and an increase in the significance of images at all levels of (post)modern society. Everything that wants to acquire meaning must become an image" (Schroer 2013: 17).

And, as Schroer also points out, visibility is by no means a good thing per se. It can certainly be intentional, for example when street musicians place themselves prominently in shopping streets. But it can also be unintentional, and not just for criminal activities. In such cases, we draw curtains in front of our windows, pull our hoods down low over our foreheads or do not give photographers permission to take pictures of us at school parties (Schroer 2013).

---

3 This newspaper article, for example, reports on the artistic actions that took place in Imti: https://www.omanobserver.om/article/1104984/oman/community/every-house-a-piece-of-art-in-imti-village-makeover, last accessed on 28.02.2024.

Fig. 1: A large picture at Muscat Airport refers to an old settlement in Misfat Al Abriyin.

In the following, we draw on these considerations and combine them with the ad hoc observations described at the beginning. Systematically, we now want to ask how Omani settlements actually become visible and what meanings they acquire in this process. At the same time, this includes the question of what is not shown. As it should have become clear by now, visibility is not a purely "objective" category; it is strongly linked to the interpretative and productive achievements of actors; the same thing does not necessarily have to be visible for two actors.

We pay particular attention to the question of how the Omani settlements come into view for *tourists*. The decision in favour of the tourist view of the settlements is not arbitrary, for two reasons. Firstly, tourism is playing an increasingly important role in Oman. It has been receiving special support for years and is intended to help provide the country with a second economic pillar alongside fossil fuels.[4] Settlements also play an important role in the course of this tourism. Large pictures of the old settlement of Misfat Al Abriyin greet you as soon as you arrive at Muscat International Airport (Fig. 1). But the settlements are not only intended to attract international visitors; domestic tourism is also increasingly focusing on marketing the settlements.[5]

---

4 The diversification of the economy also plays a key role in the "Oman Vision 2040", an action paper published in 2020 that outlines the national strategy for the next two decades. See: https://www.oman2040.om/?lang=en, last accessed on 28.02.2024.

5 Especially during the Covid-19 pandemic, domestic tourism was boosted enormously as part of the "staycation campaign". Numerous new cafés in the old settlements of Nizwa, as well as bed-and-breakfast hotels in smaller towns such as Birkat Al Mawz, Al Hamra etc. have sprung up in the last four years.

The second argument for the analysis of tourism perspectives on the settlements presented here is of a more theoretical nature. Independently of Oman, many social science publications have established that a tourism perspective can be particularly interesting for understanding specific places and sites. Both tourism and its geographical destinations are considered to be closely related to each other. In other words, tourism seeks out specific places and locations for its fulfilment, and thus sees specific aspects and characteristics in specific places. This always happens in comparison with the familiar, usually one's own origin. In other words: as tourists, we always compare our travel destinations with the places and contexts we have left behind, and we tend to look for and see the new, the unusual, and often evaluate the destinations primarily according to how different they are from our home country. From such a perspective, tourism comes into view as a medium of spatial production in which practices of cultural comparison are constitutively embedded (Pott 2015; Wöhler – Pott – Denzer 2010).

At the same time, specific locations do not remain untouched and unchanged by tourism. This goes so far that considerations regarding the tourist's idea of the attractiveness of places and districts are often already a proactive component of urban development processes today. Here we see what the British sociologist John Urry called "the tourist gaze" in the 1990s (Urry 1990). This tourist gaze seeks the difference to what is one's own and what is special, and it is clearly experiencing an increasing universalization: it is not only peculiar to those who embark on a journey, but is also anticipated by those who are visited and who strive to specifically enable this experience of difference through the design of urban and other tourist spaces. In other words, much of what can be observed today in urban reconstructions or new buildings, for example, cannot be explained without taking into account the effects that tourism generates with its search for the experience of difference and the operation of cultural comparison (e.g. Potsdamer Platz, Potsdam City Palace). In addition, and this is particularly interesting for the Omani case, such space-producing media as tourism are not free of exoticizing views. The supposed Other then becomes an exotic Other and contains orientalist attributions. However, these images are not only brought to the respective place by tourists, but are also produced by the travellers in the form of a "self-orientalism" (Feighery 2012). Orientalist perspectives are reproduced in order to fulfil the expectations of tourists.

To put it bluntly, one could say that even our own "domestic" spaces are increasingly being thought of and reshaped by the tourist gaze (everything must somehow always provide interesting motifs, be Instagrammable, etc.). None of these are purely urban phenomena. Anyone who has travelled a little through European regions in recent years could observe that they too are increasingly perceiving themselves through the eyes of potential tourist visitors and marking corresponding sights, beautiful views, etc. The example of cities such as Venice also shows how profoundly such attributions of meaning and their successful marketing can transform a city.

This is certainly relevant for Oman. There were and still are different concepts and activities as to how the settlements should be presented. At the same time, this goes back to the above considerations as to what the settlements then appear as; it is therefore not simply about their visibility, but also about the question of what is visible, which aspects of the past and thus also of today's Oman should be emphasized. Generally speaking, the built environment plays different roles and has different meanings for the social.

We use texts and images from different sources as our empirical basis. Firstly, and this forms the majority of our sample, these are posts on Instagram that were created in the old settlements and that depict the settlements in different ways. The posts are either from private travellers or from accounts that identify themselves as tourist guides. Secondly, we looked at "classic" travel guides and analysed them in term of their thematization of the settlements. In some cases, such as Lonely Planet, entries from the travel guides' websites were included in the sample in addition to the printed books. Thirdly and finally, we analysed travel blogs that addressed Oman as a travel destination. In this way, we integrated a total of 35 entries into our dataset. Without exception, these entries date from the last five years.

We then subjected this material to a qualitative-interpretative analysis. We were guided by the principles of reconstructive social research and, in particular, grounded theory (Glaser – Strauss 1967). We therefore did not examine the texts for the frequency of mentions of specific places or other terms. Rather, we were interested in the way in which the settlements were thematized in the postings and texts, which aspects were photographed, and so on. In essence, we are interested in how the Omani settlements appear from the perspective of the tourist gaze.

Settlements on Instagram and in travel guides

It is by no means the case that all *ḥārāt* appear at some point in travel guides and blogs. Rather, there is a clear hierarchy in the visibility of the settlements; in other words, some settlements are clearly privileged by the tourist gaze.

Misfat Al Abriyin is at the top of the list. This picturesque village on the slopes of Jabal Shams, not far from Nizwa, appears in many travel guides and blogs. It is also well photographed and prominently featured at Omani airports, mirror-inverted and without further explanation. Here, again, a perspective is used that shows the settlement in a kind of long shot, nestled against the mountain, surrounded by palm trees and not recognizable as deserted at first glance. Also, Al Hamra and Ibra certainly belong in this series of privileged settlements. The *ḥārāt* located in these places also frequently appear in travel guides and blogs or are recommended as other places to visit.

Such a hierarchy can also be found in the Instagram posts. Here, too, the aforementioned settlements predominate under more general hashtags such as #oman or #mudbrick; places such as Misfat Al Abryin or Al Hamra are also very frequently represented and visible on Instagram. This is hardly surprising; presumably most individual tourists also visit the sources we have researched and then determine the corresponding destinations. At the same time, it becomes clear that from a tourist's point of view, the enormous number of potentially possible destinations quickly narrows down considerably, and that websites such as travel guides and blogs play an important role here. This primarily reflects the view of the settlements from a non-Omani perspective. Among the Omani population, the level of awareness of the old settlements is certainly much broader. Most family estates have old houses, which are visited with sometimes more or sometimes lesser frequency (e.g. during special holidays or excursions). However, especially in tourist marketing aimed at a foreign audience, there is a high concentration on certain settlements such as Misfat Al Abriyin, Birkat Al Mawz or Al Hamra.

However, the visibility of the settlements is not only created on tourist websites. Local signs and signposts also play an important role. Here, too, important differences can be identified. For example, it is not uncommon for settlements to be mentioned in travel guides, but then not particularly advertised on site and difficult to find. This is the case with Imti mentioned at the beginning. Then there are the very inconspicuous settlements that have no signs and are not mentioned in travel guides, but nevertheless have interesting *ḥārāt*. And finally, at the other end of the scale, there are the settlements that are made very visible, which usually goes hand in hand with their tourist exploitation. An example of this is Birkat Al Mawz, which is pointed out at many tourist information points. On site, in a new and very professionally equipped café for tourist use, you are also offered a graphically appealing city map that shows the way to the old parts of the settlement.

In the following, however, we are not interested in these different intensities of visibility or the media, through which the settlements are publicized. Instead, we turn to the question of how the *ḥārāt* are actually shown, what role they play in the images. If you take a superficial look at the depictions of the settlements on Instagram or travel blogs, for example, there are sometimes clear differences in what is shown of the *ḥārāt* and in what way. Our analyses in this regard have revealed three different modes, which we describe in more detail below: Firstly, the *ḥārāt* act as a backdrop, secondly, they are presented in a romanticized way as ruins, and thirdly, they are the subject of a material history.

The settlements as a backdrop for tourist (self-)presentation

In the first mode identified, the settlements are not the focus of the Instagram photos, but rather play the role of a backdrop. Although they can be seen in the pictures, they play more of a supporting role. They are hardly mentioned by name or explained in any other way. Even the fact that we are dealing with abandoned settlements can go unmentioned and is not clear from the images alone.

In this mode, the ruins are important in their aesthetic dimension. They serve as part of a background or backdrop, which is usually a composition of date palm groves, mountains, blue sky and the settlements. However, the settlements are neither visually in focus, nor in the accompanying texts. There, Oman is usually mentioned in general as the location of the photograph, sometimes the city. However, this is done without reference to the specific character of the houses to be seen, an example of the "de-historicization of the ruins" observed by Martin Zimmermann (Zimmermann 2024: 12).

The settlements thus become a lifeless and passive backdrop that serves to aestheticize or otherwise represent one's own experience. This, one could argue, is also the case in other examples, such as when photos are posted with the Eiffel Tower in the background, which is rarely mentioned specifically. However, such image compositions must be distinguished from the examples mentioned in Oman. In the first case, the Eiffel Tower serves as an iconic marker of one's own location, which does not need to be named further, but from who's fame one benefits and which is important. The situation is different with the settlements; they serve as an essentially anonymous backdrop that functions solely through its aesthetics and otherwise contributes nothing genuinely unique. In short: other "beautiful" images could be posted instead of the settlements, but the Eiffel Tower is not interchangeable.

Within this mode of "the settlements as a backdrop", a distinction can be made between two types. The first has already been described in its outline. Here, the settlements are presented as part of the landscape, as if they were one with the neighbouring oases, palm trees and other features. They are not even mentioned separately, but are taken for granted and presented as part of the overall scenery. They fulfil an aesthetic function, but are only made visible to a limited extent. They are part of the images, but at the same time are not highlighted or thematized separately.[6]

In the second performance type, the settlements are also merely a backdrop, but for the presentation of the photographer's own self. The settlements then serve as a backdrop against which the account holders present themselves. The poses adopted vary. Sometimes people stand in the foreground and look directly into the camera, others adopt particular postures. In other cases, they make more contact with the settlement, take a closer look at a building or look in the direction of the settlement.[7]

The settlements are rarely described in more detail here, sometimes not even the exact location is named. Here, too, they unfold their value primarily as an aesthetically appealing, extraordinary backdrop. This is also reflected in the commentaries. Here, the photographic skills of the accounts are praised rather than the settlements being discussed.

The settlements as places of romance and mysticism

In the second mode, the settlements themselves come more into focus. This happens above all through their interpretation as ruins. This implies at least two things. Firstly, in contrast to many posts from the previously described mode, the settlements are marked as abandoned, which also explains the partially dilapidated condition of the buildings on display. Even if many questions remain unanswered or new ones can be asked, this is a more precise description of the respective places and frees them from their backdrop-like existence.

Secondly, this is often combined with a "charging" of the settlements, which other authors have described as "ruin romanticism" (Zimmermann 1989) or "fetishization" (Wilkinson 2023). The settlements are consistently described in positive terms; there is basically no criticism of the condition of the settlements or anything similar. They are described in the posts as fascinating places that exude a special atmosphere. Instead, talk about the settlements goes hand in hand with their framing as mysterious places ("fairytale villages"), which are compared to legendary places and would make an ideal location for film adaptations of Grimm's tales or a fairy tale of One Thousand and One Nights. The history of the places is not really explained; it remains deliberately diffuse and unclear (Fig. 2).

The posts that emphasize the "unbelievability" that people still lived in the places not long ago point in a similar direction. In other descriptions, the word "surreal" is used for this; this also marks the unclear affiliation of the settlements in both temporal and social terms. Apparently, they fall out of all known grids and can hardly be brought into line with the observers' "stock of knowledge" (Schütz – Luckmann 2003). The only direction of the interpretations is therefore a diffuse "back". Even if it remains unclear exactly which era this "back" takes us to, the reference to "traveling back in time" and other semantics of time travel is helpful for tourists on site to give themselves, but also the readers of their Instagram posts, an impression of the settlements.

---

6 Kristin Hesse on Instagram: On top of the roof of one of the houses in this village of ruins overlooking the architecture and date palm farm. Very surreal #oman #alhamra #gcc #thegulf #middleeast #ruins #village #rooftop #datefarm #travel #adventure #sunshine (https://www.instagram.com/p/BibnF7wnTa6/).

7 Thewayfarerreel on Instagram: Summer heat has me indoors but I miss exploring on foot // January, 2021 #muscat #oman #experienceoman #visitoman #beautyhasanaddress #travel #travelgram #misfatalabreyeen #misfat #omantourism #ruins #heritagetourism #timeoutmuscat #shotoniphone #doorsofoman #timeoutmuscat (https://www.instagram.com/p/CQ3WmTxLSgT/).

Fig. 2: The history of the places is not really explained; it is deliberately left diffuse and unclear (photograph: quaffingreilly).

For other observers, the ruins – as a form of romanticism – are a kind of adventure playground. The opportunity to explore the abandoned settlements independently is particularly appealing. It is precisely the lack of further explanation and information that makes visiting the settlements an "adventure". On the one hand, all buildings are freely accessible and therefore also areas that used to be private; on the other hand, it is almost impossible to predict what is hidden in the buildings or around the next corner. Parallels to movements such as the Urban Explorers are obvious here. In this field, too, the exploration of lost places becomes an undertaking that promises excitement and thrills, thus mystifying and romanticizing the abandoned places.

The settlements as material history

The (mere) romanticization of the settlements obviously has its blind spots or goes hand in hand with the avoidance of historical depth of focus. This becomes clear, for example, in this comment: "These ruins are so fascinating. I'd love to know more about their history." Exactly this, namely a more precise historical description and contextualization, takes place in a third mode of Instagram presentations. The settlements appear here as representatives of the past. Although these posts continue to be created by tourists and are not of a scientific origin, the settlements here become more than backdrops or romantic and adventurous places. Rather, they are material witnesses to Omani history.

The level of detail varies greatly. Sometimes it is simply stated that the ruins were once inhabited settlements. Others refer more generally to their historical value ("There is a house that tells about the impact of the past and an ancient heritage - blessed hands."). Other posts, however, also mention the age of the settlements and provide more precise information about their size: "The ancient city of Qalhat in Oman was a flourishing trade centre between 13th-14th c., a fascinating place attracting famous visitors as Marco Polo and Ibn Battuta".[8]

However, even in these cases, the reasons for the departure are very rarely stated. On the one hand, one post dispels any fears or ambiguities and "normalizes" the villages as earlier preliminary stages of living conditions: "There's nothing sinister about why they're abandoned, people have just upgraded their living situations." This counteracts the mythical charge and interpretation of the settlement; the post can thus be read as a counterpart to the second mode. At the same time, however, the excerpts themselves remain opaque. The phrase "people have just upgraded their living situations" tends to conceal the harsh break that accompanied the departure from the settlements. This is more reminiscent of classic sociological theories of modernization, which had a clear idea of worse and better ways of living and therefore only interpreted history and progress one-dimensionally.

These attempts to give the settlements historical depth are sometimes, but rarely, accompanied by errors. For example, settlements are described as the result of deliberate destruction or as being significantly older than they actually are.

The settlements as a confrontation between past and present

Finally, a fourth point should be addressed, which played a role in many posts and to a certain extent lies at odds with the modes mentioned so far. It concerns the fact that the settlements are repeatedly interpreted as a special intersection of old and new, as places where past and present meet in a specific way and can thus be experienced in their own way.

This is most obvious in those posts where tourists observe and thematize the juxtaposition of renovated and unrenovated settlements. Sometimes this constellation is then noted rather neutrally ("Wandering the historic streets of Harat Al Bilad (orig.) in Manah, Oman. While many old houses across the country are left to ruin when people move to more modern homes, the 900 year old Manah old town is being preserved, with a government initiative helping to restore the traditional buildings"). In other cases, however, the restoration or at least the protection of the ruins is demanded (or at least the lack of such protection is wondered about) in order to preserve the material past and make it accessible and tangible for present and future contemporaries.

Other posts refer to the juxtaposition of old and new using the example of houses in which, in the 1980s and 1990s, residents attempted to install electricity and new technology in the clay buildings and modernize them in this way. Ultimately, such attempts failed for various reasons, not least for structural reasons, but they can still

8 IcOnem on Instagram: The ancient city of Qalhat in Oman was a flourishing trade centre between 13th-14th c., a fascinating place attracting famous visitors as Marco Polo and Ibn Battuta. In 1507 the Portouguese fleet reaches the coast near Masirah, passes Sur and at the end takes Qalhat. The conflict leads to the destruction of the city and many of its monuments, leaving mainly ruins at its end. We are engaged in making Qalhat archaeological site living again starting with drone captures like this one joined to innovative 3D technologies. Explore our missions at http://iconem.com. #archaeology #oldstones #culturalheritage #ruins #dronestagram #unescosite #qalhat #iconem #dronepic #oman (https://www.instagram.com/p/BSJYVGkAasI/).

be seen today. This interweaving of old building fabric and new technology is then perceived as "unique".[9]

A very unique confrontation of past and present is shown in a few videos in which people cross the settlements on racing bikes. Here, as described above, the settlements serve as a backdrop, but are accentuated not least by the contrast with the modern bicycles. Here, the relationship between old and new is even more different than above: No transformation of the ruins into the present or their preservation is called for. Rather, the effect consists precisely of the dilapidated background representing the (non-technological) past, against which the protagonist presents himself as modern and up to date.

Finally, a place that is surprising for some, but pleasant for many, to find in the settlements is a café. In a whole series of cases, these have emerged in the course of (partial) renovations and new uses of the old settlements, perhaps in the greatest density in Birkat Al Mawz. For many, finding one or even several modern cafés with all of today's usual amenities in these settlements, which on the one hand appear abandoned and deserted, is an additional incentive or added value of their visit: "*Notre inoubliable coup de cœur lors de notre road trip à Oman. On avait prévu d'y faire juste un arrêt café dans le magnifique rooftop du @baitalsabah pour finalement y rester quasiment 3h*". On the one hand, the surprising contrast between old and new is emphasized and has its own value. At the same time, however, the new – and the familiar – such as the cafés act as a kind of bridge to the old and facilitate one's own stay in the abandoned settlements.

Conclusion

It is striking that the settlements, as seen through the tourist gaze on Instagram, are described as something beautiful and pleasant in almost all cases. Hardly anyone complains about their existence or finds their presence disturbing. Instead, their touristic value is often emphasized, often with the emphasis that the settlements are not mentioned in every travel guide and are therefore "off the beaten track". The responses to such posts are also mostly supportive and share the enthusiasm. Rather than criticizing the ruins, it is pointed out that they should be better protected. They are obviously attributed a value that emphasizes the cultural and historical significance that is apparently inherent in the old houses.

In light of this finding, it only makes sense that some settlements have been and are being restored, both now and in the recent past. In cases such as Manah, this concerns the entire *ḥāra*; in other cities such as Nizwa or Ibra, the renovation of old buildings is intertwined with the construction of completely new houses. However, the old buildings and settlements clearly have the potential to act as tourist attractions. At the moment, the attraction of the settlements seems to stem primarily from the fact that at least some, if not all, of the buildings are in a state of abandonment and partial decay. If this is combined with newly established cafés – all the better. But the state of ruin is always preferred in the posts.

These ruins, as is also clear from the pictures, are seen and staged from a specific perspective, whereby much remains hidden and is not visible, because there is a lot that cannot be seen in the pictures. These include areas that are used for dumping garbage,

9 Experienceoman on Instagram (image credit: @temporaryvagabond): What makes Ruins of Al Hamra unique is the blending of the old and new. Mixed in with the mud and wood houses are some slightly newer ones, with electric lights and coils of wire visible from time to time. The ruins are just a 2 hour drive from Muscat and injects variety to your itinerary. #BeautyHasAnAddress #ExperienceOman #Oman (https://www.instagram.com/p/Bg5-qHuDPwL).

where animal carcasses can be found, or the houses that are actually still used by the descendants of the original owners as shelter and storage space and are usually fitted with new doors and locked. The rather "clean ruins" are therefore presented and/or perceived.

Added to this is the conspicuous absence of images or videos in which the settlements are presented as threatening or sinister. This marks a notable difference to a phenomenon known as "dark tourism" (Stone – Hartmann – Seaton 2018). Tourists deliberately head for places that do not appear pleasant and inviting on the surface. The most prominent example of this movement is driving and visiting the area around the former Chernobyl nuclear power plant. But it also includes exploring abandoned factories or ghost towns in the west of the USA.

Instead, you are more likely to find videos in which the settlements are staged for advertising purposes. These are posts in which, for example, a settlement is depicted and the description then includes contact details and information about a bookable tour to this location; however, none of this has a gruesome appeal, but only entices with pleasant experiences. The posts by Clive Gracey, who uses elements and details of the settlements artistically in his pictures and then offers them commercially (e.g. Doors of Oman), also aim in this direction.

Overall, we are dealing here with a view of the Omani mudbrick settlements that is decidedly positive and benevolent. Although there are differences in terms of historical depth and the classification of the settlements, they are marked as worth seeing, aesthetically pleasing and special.

At the same time, this view remains very open. The Omani settlements do not have "one" dominant interpretation, they are not seen as a symbol of decline or decay, they are not a reminder of wars (only in exceptional cases, such as in the ruins of Tanuf, but even that is generally little known) or natural disasters, etc. This also makes them into surfaces of projection or places of self-staging for an aesthetically pleasing photo in front of the picturesque assemblage of ruined houses, date groves and the cloudless sky. Within the broad field of lost cities and their reception, they thus represent a remarkable case, as they are not – as is often the case – interpreted as a symbol of decline or decay (see Zimmermann 2017).

Much will now depend on how the settlements are treated in the future. Wind and weather are taking their toll on the materials; without intervention and protective measures, the settlements will gradually disappear. At the same time, such measures change the character of the settlements, sometimes decisively. This can be seen in Misfat Al Abriyin, for example, which can hardly be described as a deserted place, but is full of colourful signs and advertisements for cafés and guest houses. This example in particular shows the influence that tourism can have on settlements and the traces it leaves behind. Either way, the abandoned settlements live on, changing their form and also their use.

References

Bauer, C. – Dolgan, C. 2020
Towards a definition of lost places, *ERDKUNDE* 74/2, 101–115. DOI: 10.3112/erdkunde.2020.02.02

Brighenti, A. 2007
Visibility: A category for the social sciences, *Current Sociology* 55/ 3, 323–342. DOI: 10.1177/0011392107076079

Feighery, W. G. 2012
Tourism and self-orientalism in Oman: A critical discourse analysis, *Critical Discourse Studies* 9/3, 269–284. DOI: 10.1080/17405904.2012.688210

Glaser, B. – Strauss, A. 1967
The discovery of grounded theory. Strategies for qualitative research, Chicago.

Pott, A. 2015
Places of tourism. A spatial and social theory study, Bielefeld.

Schroer, M. 2013
Visible or invisible? The battle for attention in visual culture, *Social World* 64/1–2, 17–36. DOI: 10.1111/jtsb.12038

Stone, P. R. – Hartmann, R. – Seaton, A. (eds) 2018
The Palgrave handbook of dark tourism studies, Cambridge.

Urry, J. 1990
The tourist gaze, London.

Schütz, A. – Luckmann, T. 2003
Structures of the lifeworld, Constance.

Wilkinson, T. 2023
Life in ruins. The fetishization of decay in contemporary architecture, in: J. O. Habeck – F. Schmitz (eds): *Ruins and forgotten places*, Bielefeld, 91–105.

Wöhler, K. – Pott, A. – Denzer, V. (eds) 2010
Tourism spaces. On the sociostructural construction of a global phenomenon, Bielefeld.

Zimmermann, M. 2017
Lost cities, urban explorers and ancient landscapes: On living with ruins, in: S. Müller – A. Selbitschka (eds), *Beyond the everyday: Festschrift for Thomas O. Höllmann on his 65th birthday*, Wiesbaden, 297–312.

Zimmermann, M. (ed.) 2024
Lost Cities. On living with abandoned cities in the cultures of the world, Munich.

Zimmermann, R. 1989
Artificial ruins. Studies on their meaning and form, Wiesbaden.

Modern Architecture vs "Pre-modern" *Ḥārāt*

Architecture Against the Tribes in Oman

Heike Delitz

"Architecture against the tribes". Introduction

The most instructive question which *ḥārāt* in contemporary Oman offers for a sociological – and architectural sociological – perspective is perhaps the following: why is there a spectacular contrast between those decaying quarters on the one side, and the modern infrastructural and architectural artefacts next to them, on the other side? What was the social logic of this traditional architecture, which the *ḥārāt* are; and what is the social logic of this double architectural constellation of today? In suggesting an answer, searching the social function of the respective architectures, I describe and theorize about the architecture or built environment, and more precisely architectural cultures (that is, all built structures, but also woven or sewn forms of architecture, in their structural differences), as "architectural modes of collective existence" (Delitz 2018): Architecture contributes to the cultural institution of societies or of modes of collective lives. Architecturally, social inequalities are instituted; a relation between nature and culture is established and made durable; a particular history is visually present, or differentiations and separations of social functions, or between genders are introduced, together and parallel to the institution of the social within discourses, for instance. At the same time, architecture also correlates to, and in some cases, forces societal transformations. This seems particularly true in the case of colonial architectural politics (for Algeria, see Bourdieu – Sayad 2020). "Architectural cultures" – institutionalized ensembles of the built environment and infrastructure (with their use of particular materials, with the different dimensions of the respective built, or woven, artefacts; with different modes of their relation to the ground, or with the particular ways in which a history is made visible and intelligible) – are modes of the cultural institution and transformation of society.

It is in this context that the following article suggests interpreting Oman's traditional architecture – the *ḥārāt* quarters – as an institution of a particular mode of collective existence, namely a tribal society, and to understand the introduction of a modern architectural culture as architectural politics of the transformation of this mode of society. Or, since the 1970s, the

in: S. Döpper – B. Mershen – J. Kanditt – I. Biezeveld – T. Schmidt-Lux (eds) 2025, *Mudbrick Settlements of the Oman Peninsula. Inhabited – Abandoned – Re(dis)covered*, Leiden: Sidestone Press, 133–146.

hegemonic politics of the nation-state Oman means a purposeful transformation of the tribal mode of collective existence, in the mode of architecture. This argument has three parts. After introducing the term "architectural modes of collective life" as the task of the first part, the second part follows Thibault Klinger's *L'Oman contemporain. Aménagement du territoire et identité nationale* (Klinger 2021).[1] Klinger – and with him the following article – understands the architectural and infrastructural politics of Sultan Qaboos since the 1970s as a mode of the institution of the nation-state, or a national collective identity – beneath, and through the desire for "modern" houses and more comfort. The transformation of both the territory and the built environment (the building of new houses, of quarters,[2] and of infrastructure, immediately next to the decaying *ḥārāt*), and additionally, a new politics of tourism which today conserves the *ḥārāt* in the name of being Omani cultural heritage – are politics-against-the-tribes by the means of architecture. The massif uprooting and resettlement, the "massive abandonment of the traditional habitat" and its substitution by new architecture, are intended to "neutralise the territorial base of tribal power", and to imagine a national identity which overwrites the tribal loyalties (Klinger 2021: 114). And if the modern state of Oman in this way, in the 1970s, "begun with a politics of the transformation of the territory", the "branding" of Oman today is a second politics in the name of the nation-state (Klinger 2019: 2021), and against the tribal organization of society. In seeing the nation-state in this way as politics "against", as being the counterpart of a tribal institution of society (and vice versa), the third part of the argument will introduce the political anthropology of Pierre Clastres. Although he himself actually focused on other societies (Amerindian ones), this political anthropology is instructive for three narrowly linked reasons: Firstly, Clastres offers a general theory of the political institution of society; secondly, Clastres is a pioneer in the "permanent exercise in the decolonization" of anthropological (and sociological) thought (Viveiros de Castro 2014: 39); and thirdly, Clastres offers a theory of a "tribal" mode of the institution of society, a mode for which sociological and political theory tends to think in inadequate, Eurocentric and evolutionist notions, as being pre-modern and archaic; in short: a past mode of the institution of society. With Pierre Clastres in contrast, *ḥārāt* can be interpreted as architecturally instituting a tribal society, or a "society-against-the-state". A tribal society is not the pre-modern forerunner, but it is the counterpart of a national society. If the *ḥāra* was architecturally instituting a society-against-the-state, Oman's modern architecture since the 1970s in turn becomes intelligible as being an architecture-against-the-tribe. The new, small, and uniform houses in the neighbourhood of the *ḥārāt*; the infrastructural restructuring of the whole territory; the massive resettlement; the destruction or the decay of the old quarters; and, finally, their branding as being Omani cultural heritage, all these architectural facts serve as national politics. Their purpose is the institution of the imagination of the nation, of a shared identity of all Omanis – instead of the bifurcation of identities, which is the feature of a tribal organization of society. And even the spectacle of the decaying *ḥārāt* is politics against the tribes, for it represents this tribal architecture and society as being pre-modern, as being the precursor of the nation-state. It is also to avoid such ideas (of the tribal as a pre-modern mode of society) that I will firstly consider Oman's architectural politics since the 1970s; and only after that will I come to tribal society and architecture.

---

1 All translations from French are made by the author.

2 For social houses projects – with 15,000 new residential buildings – see for instance Klinger 2021: 92–93.

"Architectural modes of collective existence". Theory for the Social Positivity of Architecture

Introducing the formula "architectural mode of collective existence" (Delitz, 2018), the first clarification consists of saying that the notion "architecture" here refers to the entire built environment, and also to woven or sewn architecture (tents, yurts), to interior design, and to settlement patterns and infrastructure (for such a broad notion of architecture see Cache, 1995). Equally important, the notion of architecture is not restricted to the profession of architect; it includes vernacular architecture, particularly. Understanding architecture as a "mode of collective existence", then, implies the refusal to see architecture as being a mirror, a representation or an expression of the social. Rather, I want to think that *within* architecture, *architecturally*, the social is instituted. The social positivity of architecture, of course, is intertwined with discourses and other symbolic systems in the way of a mutual overdetermination (as Louis Althusser would have said). The particular positivity of architecture as material culture lies in creating visibilities of bodies and of their movements, of creating affects, of enabling and shaping interactions. Furthermore, the built environment *is* the visual and the spatial figure of the society or collective; it is a mode of instituting a collective identity, and it makes the (otherwise invisible) collective or society intelligible. Social inequalities (between gender and generations) also are instituted architecturally, too (beneath discourses). The same is to be said for the relation between nature and culture, or for the relation between social institutions (economic, political, religious ones, etc.). Architecture not as mirror, but as a mode of the institution of the social: the theory of society which underlies this formula is the postfoundational theory of *society as imaginary institution* (Castoriadis 1997). According to this clarification of the notion of society, society – being never a whole and never an unity, nor being an identity – is to be thought of as an imaginary institution, i.e. as an imaginary fixation of the collective; as an imagination of unity; and as an imagination-based division of humans, of living beings and of all things. On one side, this allows us to think about the institution of (for instance, religious) *subjects*. Their deepest desires, their daily actions and interactions, their normative convictions, etc., are instituted in the religious symbolic system and its imaginary foundation on "God" (*cf.* Castoriadis 1997: 140–141). On the other side, Castoriadis stresses such imaginary institutions which refer to a founding Other (God) as "society's alienation with respect to itself" (Castoriadis 1997: 214), or as a heteronomous institution of society (Castoriadis 1997: 372–373). With the systems of imaginary institutions, founded in a first, or a primary, or a "central signification",

> "[e]verything occurs as if the ground where the creativity of society is manifested in the most tangible way, the ground on which it acts, brings into existence and makes itself exist in bringing into existence, had to be covered over by an imaginary creation arranged in such a way as to allow society to conceal what it is to itself [...]. Everything happens as if society were unable to recognize itself as making itself, as instituting itself, as selfinstituting" (Castoriadis 1997: 213).

Therefore, the primary or central signification ("God", or, in nation-states, the "Nation") functions as a founding Other. This imagined being, the source of the collective's identity and unity, ensures "the organization of signifiers and signifieds into a system" (Castoriadis 1997: 140). Being fully imaginary, God (or the Nation) "denote[s] nothing at all", and "connote[s] just about everything" (Castoriadis 1997: 143). It is in this way that Castoriadis suggests seeing in collective life "the union and the tension of instituting society and of instituted society" (Castoriadis 1997: 108). If society is an imaginary institution, it "has to use the symbolic", "not only to 'express' itself [...] but to 'exist'" (Castoriadis 1997: 127). Material culture, and inter alia architecture, is in this way active or positive *modes* of collective existence. They offer the most spacious of those visible "figures" of which the social institution consists. For, if the "social historical is a perpetual flux of self-alteration", any society has to provide "itself with 'stable' figures by which it makes itself visible, visible to and for itself as well" (Castoriadis 1997: 204).

A similar cultural theory of society is already to be found in the work of Claude Lévi-Strauss. In order to see architecture as a cultural mode of collective existence this work is important for two reasons. Firstly, Lévi-Strauss forces us to think of "society" as being of "symbolic origin" (Lévi-Strauss 1987: 21), as being culturally instituted, and as being instituted in meaning systems. The central thesis concerning classificatory meaning systems is: The "category of class and the notion of opposition" – in totemic classifications for instance – "are utilized by the social order in its formation" (Lévi-Strauss 1991: 97). In short, no "social phenomenon may be explained, [...] if symbolism is not set up as an *a priori* requirement" (Lévi-Strauss 1945: 517–518). And secondly, Lévi-Strauss' structural anthropology foregrounds the comparative interest in *different* modes of collective existence (like the nation-state versus the tribal mode of collective life), thereby carefully avoiding any evolutionist notion for extra-European cultures and societies as being pre-modern ones. Structural anthropology aims "to be less Ethnocentrist as possible" (Descola – Kirsch 2008: 33) in seeing the global cultures or societies as being contemporary to each other, as being "groups of transformations" (*cf.* inter alia Lévi-Strauss 1966: 89–90), i.e. *versions* or *variants* of each other. It is in his tradition (though not uncritically), that Pierre Clastres (1989; 2010, see below) unfolds the notion of "primitive" societies, of tribal societies as being "societies-against-the-state" – instead of seeing those modes of collective life as societies without a state or as being pre-state societies.

Comparing different architectural modes of collective existence (or different architectural cultures) worldwide, I am following structural anthropology in its aim to be as non-Eurocentric as possible (non-evolutionist as possible). Furthermore, based on such a synchronic comparison of collective modes and/or of cultural systems, it is this tradition of anthropological thought which then allows us to see the transformative effects of architecture: transformations of collective lives which are caused by colonial or neo-colonial architecture, for instance. In the case of Oman, the question would be, which social transformations have modern buildings and infrastructure since 1970 caused, or at least, which of such social transformations were intended with the introduction of the new, modern urbanism?[3] "One of the fundamental tasks of the State is to striate the space [...], or to utilize smooth spaces as a means of communication in the service of striated space", we read in Deleuze and Guattari (1997: 385), and also: "One could also speak of deterritorialization, since the earth becomes an object" (of property rights, ibid.). In the case of Oman, two different modes of collective life – but both being tribal modes – are affected by, and aimed at by the Sultan's state policy: namely, the sedentary and the nomadic tribes within the territory of the state.

3 For a similar case study on "new Islamic urbanism" (related to the architectural politics of the monarchy of Saudi Arabia) see Maneval 2019.

Architectural Modernization since the 1970s: Architecture against the tribes

> "[D]ominated by residential buildings in a landscape of infinite urban expansion, Oman's space embodies a politics of modernisation, not without posing questions in view of the decaying *ḥārāt*", writes Thibault Klinger (2021: 152).

Modern architecture on the one side, and seemingly pre-modern, archaic *ḥārāt* on the other side: it is this constellation between two different architectural modes which institutes a new and particular political reality, that of "the most absolute monarchy" of the region (Klinger 2021: 27), which thinks of itself in the notion of the "nation". In order to create this new collective reality (as an imaginary institution), several architectural policies are playing together: the infra-structuration of the territory; the clusters of new, "modern" residential buildings alongside the highways, each on a small parcel of land; the uprooting and the resettlement of large parts of the population; massive immigration – such architectural and political tendencies serve to *give the new state* a distinct "Omani" identity, and at the same time a homogenous character.

With the new spatial structure and new residential buildings, Qaboos promised a "pacification" of the whole society: it is "part of his policy of modernisation", promising "peace", "not any longer as guaranteed by the walls of the *hārāt*, but as resulting from the massive uprooting, dissolving the people from the traditional houses and the *hārāt*", at the same time isolating the families in the new, isolated houses. The "new urban space knows no visible limit", as "if there are no more quarters, but only one gigantic single space." (Klinger 2021: 156). In other words, in regards to the modern architecture and infrastructure, the new space is intended to dissolve the tribes, not least in the collective and individual imagination. Furthermore, Qaboos presented the new architecture as serving security, or "counter-insecurity" (Klinger 2021: 151).

> "The layout of the territory is a geo-politics. Its main tool is the house, built on a normed parcel [...] and with financial support from the State [...]. This distinguishes Oman from other nations in the region: The rapid modernisation of the landscape and the new urban space manifest an extraordinary spatial justice, which also allowed the massive uprooting of the population in order to pacify the society and to neutralize the identification with 'problematic' places [...]. Additionally, urbanisation is a tool of political control [...]. The norms for the individual house and the new architecture are far away from those of the old habitat" (Klinger 2021: 151).

If the *ḥāra* itself has been an architectural mode of territorial control (as will be shown later), so is its decay. Or, while the new settlements and infrastructure are the visible figure of the new imaginary institution of society (the imagined nation-state of Oman), the tribal architecture of the *hārāt* is – in its ruined status – only intelligible as a pre-modern one. With the decaying quarters, a tribal society is imagined as pre-modern, as preceding the nation-state. Or, modern architecture and infrastructure are far away to be a question of "comfort" alone, although many inhabitants will explain their abandonment of the *hārāt* in those words. It is a question of comfort, but also an architectural politics against the tribes, these counterparts of a central power and an imagined national identity. In short, the *spectacle* of the decaying *hārāt* immediately next to the modern houses and routes is intended to dissolve identifications. The same could be true for the touristic revival of some *hārāt*: Their conservation (the touristic branding as national heritage, as being the "origin" of Oman, and as being a witness of the tribes as precursors of the nation-state) again cause the imagination of the tribes as being a pre-modern mode of collective life, and as being a pre-state mode. Architecture against the tribes, this seems the continuity, in which also the reduction of the number of mosques around the *ḥārāt* fit. In the context of the regrouping of the population, new mosques have been built without any relationship to the tribes. If the mosque alongside the *sabla* was the "second type of architecture emblematic of the social regulation of the *ḥārāt*, a 'decontextualisation' can again be observed" (Klinger, 2021: 198). The new mosques, too, serve to imaginarily institute *a national* collective identity (in their new location; in a new aesthetics; with new architectural elements; and in their names (Klinger 2021: 198-223). In short, a complex architectural politics was directed against the sedentary (*ḥaḍarī*, *cf.* Klinger 2021: for instance 309–310) tribes; as well as against the tribes in general.

Politics against the tribes in general: the case of the nomadic tribes

In interpreting the tribal mode of collective existence as a *counterpart* of the state, and correspondingly, seeing the architectural culture of the *ḥārāt* as *architecture-against-the-state*, further collectives and architecture should not be ignored. Aiming to establish a modern nation-state, the policy of Sultan Qaboos was not only directed against the sedentary *ḥaḍarī* tribes. Equally, and even more intensely, it was directed against the nomadic *badu* tribes. Against these tribes, the state policy aimed "to create a landscape in the desert that attempted to reproduce the settled, 'civilized' landscapes they were familiar with in the coastal and mountain valley settlement" (Chatty 2013: 139). In both cases, architecture and infrastructure play a central role: modern architecture and infrastructure, on the one side, as *architecture-against-the-tribe*, and the two traditional architectural cultures (the tents and the *ḥārat*) on the other side, as *architecture-against-the-state*. A politics of territorial control and of resettlement and a politics of sedentarization or territorialization particularly affects the nomadic *badu* tribes (the *Ḥārasis*, *Wahiba*, *Duru* and *Janaba*, Chatty 2013: 136). Indeed, in a more intense manner than the sedentary tribes, they are presented as being from a pre-modern, and additionally a "more primitive" past (Bandyopadhyay 2011: 199). Being nomads, these tribes are addressed as being "backward" – particularly the nomads who are "relegated to the 'moral margins' of societal life" (Chatty 2012: 177, with Paul Dresch). The "*Ḥārasiis* tribe clearly represent the most excluded" (Chatty 2012: 182). In the modern nation-state, expatriates now became "insiders", while the nomads in turn are the subaltern of today (Chatty 2012: 177). Such hegemony has a long history, already exerted by oil companies before 1970. The hegemony of the settled collectives and the nation-state over nomadic collectives is again not least achieved architecturally. The nomads are dislocated, displaced and centralized, or territorialized: "[S]helter and housing were particularly problematic, as government officials and ministers could not conceive of the desert being occupied in any other way than in permanent village settlements" (Chatty 2012: 186), and in any other way than with permanent infrastructure (such as pipelines, beneath routes).

> "A slow and gradual process of dislocation is taking place, based on the oil companies' unwillingness to recognise the authenticity of the *Ḥāra-siis* seasonal presence on their traditional grazing lands. This is followed by a process of displacement that is gradually forcing some *Ḥārasiis* of their lands altogether and into shabby and crowded government low cost housing" (Chatty 2012: 188).

The "authentic" desert is now presented as being *one* element of Oman's identity, hereby understood as "a pristine landscape" (Chatty 2012: 189), beneath two further core elements of the nation, namely the (decontextualized) forts of the *ḥārāt* on the one side, and the palms on the other side. "For Qaboos, particularly the forts are the signs of (his) power, they are presented as forming a landscape which unifies the nation" (Klinger 2019). In this imaginary institution of society, the *badu* tribes are also architecturally excluded: With the imagined nation (instead of the plurality of tribes) and with the institution of the *ḥāra* as being *national* heritage, the tribal mode of collective existence in general is targeted; and with "much of the building in place" (Chatty 2012: 190), and the correlated idea of the "untouched" desert, more specifically the nomadic tribes are affected.

The *ḥārāt* as architectural institution of a tribal society (architecture-against-the-State)

> "Even in societies in which the political institution is absent [...], even there the political is present, even there the question of power is posed: not in the misleading sense of wanting to account for an impossible absence, but in the contrary sense whereby, perhaps mysteriously, something exists within the absence" (Clastres 1989: 21-22).

In order to understand these formulas (architecture-against-the-tribe, architecture-against-the-state); and in order to see the positivity of the *ḥāra*, introducing the political anthropology of the already mentioned political anthropologist Pierre Clastres is overdue. A pupil of Claude Lévi-Strauss, he was an expert on Amerindian societies, as well as the author of a general theory of society, published within the two anthologies *Society against the State* (1989, French original 1974) and *Archaeology of Violence* (2010, French original 1980).

The political anthropology of Pierre Clastres

It is Pierre Clastres who allows us to understand a tribal society as a particular political institution of society – as the counterpart of a nation-state. The central aim of Clastres is to force anthropology to take extra-European societies "*seriously*", "in all their dimensions: the political dimension included, ev*en and especially when the latter is experienced* [...] *as the negation*" of the anthropologist's mode of social life (Clastres 1989: 19, final italics added). In order to do this, it is most "imperative" for anthropological theory "to accept the idea that negation does not signify nothingness; that when the mirror does not reflect our own likeness, it does not prove there is nothing to perceive" (Clastres 1989: 19). There is much to be seen in Indigenous societies, and the prerequisite is to avoid negative notions, which are inevitably Eurocentric ones: In seeing those societies particularly as societies *without* a state; or as being pre-state societies makes them nothing other than minor versions of the anthropologist's own European society. Or, the "factual judgment, adequate in itself" – a tribal society is a society *without* a state – always "hides a value judgment", namely, that those "societies are missing something – the State" (Clastres 1989: 189), that they are pre-modern societies which have to unfold a state, still. (Qaboos, "heritier d'un territoire sans Etat", writes for instance Marc Valeri 2007: 13) According to Clastres, the social logic of tribal societies "is not to be sought in that direction", it is not to sought negatively – as if those societies are missing somewhat what 'we' have (Clastres, 1989: 189–190). In order to understand this mode of the political institution of society, and therewith *the institution of society in general*, a "Copernican revolution" is needed (Clastres 1989: 25). If anthropological theory has let "primitive" societies (which means *undivided* ones) "revolve around Western civilization", then the discipline "must effect a 'heliocentric' conversion: it will then perhaps succeed in better understanding the world of others, and consequently our own" (Clastres 1989: 25–26). According to Clastres' epistemological politics, it is most imperative to substitute negative notions by positive ones. Societies "without" a state *refuse* this mode of the institution of society – they "have" a state, but in latency, virtually, institutionally avoiding its actualization by ritualized conflicts or by a *culture of war*. It is the tribal structure which institutes a centrifugal logic, or a logic of "dispersion" in contrast to the unification by a state (Clastres 2010: 273–274). Tribal conflicts are not societal accidents; rather, rivalries are constitutive for this mode of collective existence. Or, war is a *structure* of a tribal society; it is the "mode of [its] existence", for a tribal society is per definition "made up of equal, free and independent sociopolitical units". If "enemies did not exist, they would have to be invented" (Clastres 2010: 273). *Per definition*, tribal societies entail tribal alliances, and equally they entail rivalries. Dispersion, bifurcation – a tribal society reveals a logic according to which each "community, to consider itself as singular totality, needs the opposite" (Clastres 2010: 263). In short, tribal societies are *societies-against-the-state*. Institutionally they refuse a central organization and unification of the territory. Within this mode of collective existence, it is "impossible to unify [...] the multifarious variety of the tribes" (Clastres 1989: 216–217). Or, thanks to the rivalries, a tribal society follows a logic of the "parcelling" of groups and federations. The state in contrast has "to refuse the multiple". It is governed by the "horror of difference":

> "The State considers itself and proclaims itself the center of society, the whole of the social body, the absolute master of this body's various organs. Thus we discover at the very heart of the State's substance the active power of One, the inclination to refuse the multiple, the fear and horror of difference" (Clastres 2010: 108).

> "What is the State? It is the total sign of division in society, in that it is a separate organ of political power: society is henceforth divided into those who exercise power and those who submit to it [...]. Social division and the emergence of the State are the death of primitive society" (Clastres 2010: 274).

The *ḥāra* as architecture-against-the-state

Although Clastres unfolds this argument for Amerindian societies particularly (the Tupi-Guarani, the Yanomami, and other Amazonian collectives), he offers a theory of tribal societies *in general*. And although he does not mention architecture[4] – but rather the Indian chieftainship as instituting a "non-coercive political power" (Clastres 1989: 23, 205-207) and

4 For a case study of "architecture-against-the-state" see Strother 2004 (Central Africa); or Delitz 2020 (for South America).

a metaphysics according to which the "One" is the evil (Clastres 1989: 216) – this political anthropology allows us to see the political positivity of architecture, too. Following the argument of Clastres, the *ḥāra* can be seen as *instituting* (and not only mirroring) a tribal mode of collective existence. So, in which way can the *ḥārāt* (as a particular ensemble of buildings and of infrastructural artefacts, but also as a spatial structure or as a mode of territorialisation) be understood as a mode of collective existence? If a tribal society institutes a non-hierarchical mode of political organization (in contrast to the rigid social hierarchy within the tribe), if the tribes or the federations of tribes are not subject to a central power, as daily politics is the conflict, the fortification of the *ḥāra* is maybe the most important architectural detail. The walls and the towers are key in the institution of the tribal society.[5] As the *ḥāra* "is a spatial unit which encloses dwellings and communal structures belonging to one tribe and groups affiliated to it" (Mershen 1998: 201), the assembling hall (*sabla*) is also key for the institution of the tribes, for it is the place for decisions of the affairs of a tribe, or of a tribal section. "The possession of a *sabla* reflects the demographic, political, economic and social power or superiority of a tribe within the settlement" (Klinger 2021: 190). As most groupings "had their own *sabla*, a large number would thus point to a multi-tribal settlement" (Mershen 1998: 206).[6] The same is true for the number and the location of the mosques (see Mershen 1998: 207), with their ablution facilities for ritual purity, particularly in cases of contact with others, and with nomads (Bandyopadhyay 2011: 201).[7] If until 1970 this society was mainly structured by the opposition between two tribal confederations (*Hināwī* and *Ghāfirī*), their respective *ḥārāt* and the installation of a no man's land in-between was also key. The same is to be said for the localization of the tribes within the *ḥārat* (Bandyopadhyay 2004; 2005; 2011; Klinger 2021); and for the subordination of slaves and subordinated tribes, or the non-tribal Mawali population under tribal patronage – being either located within, or beyond the fortification. In Manah, there is a "clear cut spatial division" specifically "between houses of tribal population, and Mawali, non-tribal population" (Mershen 1998: 207). Furthermore, a *ḥāra* can be dominated by one tribe, or by one confederation of tribes (Klinger 2021: 181–182 mentions Al Saybani at Birkat Al Mawz). A *ḥāra* can also present "a tribal group within an ensemble, dominated by an adversary tribe and separated by a fort" (Al Yaman at Izkī; *cf.* also Bandyopadhyay 2011: 153–154). A third type is a "cosmopolitan" *ḥāra* which assembles even tribes of hostile confederations (Fanja, Manah), instituting a "supra-tribal collective identity" (Klinger 2021: 182). Here, architecturally, the *falaj* system is key (this is the most important infrastructure which was also used by Qaboos for imagining a national identity), as it requires cooperation. "The *falaj* lies in the core of the Omani identity, due to its unifying role" (Klinger 2021: 182). At the same time, the irrigation system "favoured strong tribal structures" (Siegfried 2005: 192; *cf.* Bandyopadhyay – Mershen 2022), inter alia by using water as a source of "coercion during times of political and tribal strife and

---

5 According to Birgit Mershen (1998: 206), "inhabitants stress the threat of raids by bedouins or tribal enemies. The Harat shows defensive structures, gates closed during the night, towers with canons, fortresses".

6 There are further details to be reported: for instance, small appendixes of the *sabla*, "secret rooms" (Mershen 1998: 206).

7 There are of course further social categorizations to mention, especially of the genders (for instance, in Harat al-Bilad in Manah the spatial "division between female upper and male lower floor levels", "women used the roofs for access to neighbouring houses instead of entering the public space of the streets", Mershen 1998: 208).

warfare" (Bandyopadhyay 2011: 190). Excluded from this imaginary institution of society are all non-tribal populations. In short, the tribal mode – tribal affiliations as well as hierarchies – is not only, but also *architecturally instituted*, by the structuring of visibilities and of bodily movements by built artefacts; in the built and therefore visible and durable classification of human (and nonhuman) beings and things.

Resettlement, uprooting, re-imagining: Architectural politics against the tribes

> "By systematically imposing an identical organization of dwelling, even in the most remote regions (hence the most favorable for engaging in revolutionary warfare), the forced resettlement enterprise pushed forward a homogenization of Algerian society" (Bourdieu – Sayad 2020: 15).

> "The construction of a coherent Omani territory is enabled by Qābūs' use of the house as a strategic tool, the massive uprooting which consequences on the national identity are deepest, even when continuities exist. The spectacle of the decaying traditional houses [...] contrasts with the new buildings" (Klinger 2021: 152).

Compared with the situation which Bourdieu and Sayad made visible for the French politics against the Algerian peasants, the resettlement of the tribal population in Oman was surely less forced. Nevertheless, it had similar intentions and effects: It detached the tribal structures from the territory, it delinked daily bodily movements and perceptions, and the visual figure of society from its tribal bases. At the same time, it gave the tribal structure the representation as being the pre-modern, archaic Oman – a society of a preceding past. Further tendencies are to be mentioned in this context: While in the 1970s mentioning of the *ḥāra* was a kind of taboo (Valeri 2007: 236, Klinger 2021: 181), today there are official publications which present the distribution of tribes within particular *ḥārāt*. In preserving some of them, in the "heritage turn" of politics, they are now presented as being the *Original Oman*. In other words, the spectacle of the decaying *ḥārāt* on the one side, and the spectacle of a cultural heritage on the other side, are both tools to imaginarily institute a national identity which not only overwrites tribal affiliations, but also presents them as preceding it. This is not the last word in history. In the context of decreasing welfare and due to the instable historical legitimacy of the Sultanate there seems to also be a "repolarization" of society (Valeri 2007: 469, 475–476) alongside new lines of difference (economic classes), but also alongside tribal classifications.

References

Bandyopadhyay, S. 2004
Ḥārat al Bilad (Manah): Tribal pattern, settlement structure and architecture, *The Journal of Oman Studies* 13, 183–259.

Bandyopadhyay, S. 2005
Diversity in unity: An analysis of the settlement structure of Ḥārat al-ʿAqr, Nizwā (Oman), *Proceedings of the Seminar for Arabian Studies* 35, 19–36.

Bandyopadhyay, S. 2011
Manah: An Omani oasis, an Arabian legacy architecture and social history of an Omani settlement, Liverpool.

Bandyopadhyay, S. – Mershen, B. 2022
Falaj communities in Oman: A case for local governance? *Ibadī* legal rulings and spatial and ethnohistorical observations, *Journal of Material Cultures in the Muslim World* 3/1, 6–47. DOI:10.1163/26666286-12340028

Bourdieu, P. – Sayad, A. 2020 [1964]
Uprooting. The crisis of traditional agriculture in Algeria, Cambridge.

Castoriadis, C. 1997 [1975]
The imaginary institution of society, Cambridge.

Chatty, D. 1996
Mobile pastoralists – Development, planning and social change in Oman, New York.

Chatty, D. 2012
Authenticity in the desert landscapes of Oman, in: L. Mol – T. Sternberg (eds), *Changing deserts. Integrating people and their environment*, Cambridge, 176–192.

Chatty, D. 2013
Negotiating authenticity and translocality in Oman: The "desertscapes" of the Ḥārasiis tribe, in: S. Wippel (ed.), *Regionalizing Oman: Political, economic and social dynamics*, Dordrecht, 129–145.

Chatty, D. 2016
Heritage policies, tourism and pastoral groups in the Sultanate of Oman, *Nomadic Peoples* 20/2, 200–215. http://www.jstor.org/stable/24772918.

Clastres, P. 1989 [1974]
Society against the state. Essays in political anthropology, New York.

Clastres, P. 2010 [1980]
Archaeology of violence, Los Angeles.

Deleuze, G. – Guattari, F. 1997 [1980]
A thousand plateaus. Capitalism and schizophrenia, Minneapolis.

Delitz, H. 2018
Architectural modes of collective existence, *Cultural sociology* 12/1, 37–57.
DOI: 10.1177/1749975517718435

Delitz, H. 2020
Gesellschaften der Hütten (sociétés à maisons), in: K. Krauthausen – R. Ladewig (eds), *Modell Hütte. Von emergenten Strukturen, schützender Haut und gebauter Umwelt*, Zürich, 103–128.

Descola, P. – Kirsch, M. 2008
Lévi-Strauss vu par Philippe Descola. *La lettre du Collège de France*, Hors-série 2, 29--33.
DOI: 10.4000/lettre-cdf.219

Eickelman, D. F. 1990
Identité nationale et discours religieux en Oman, in: G. Kepel – Y. Richard (eds), *Intellectuels et militants de l'Islam contemporain*, Paris, 103–128.

Klinger, T. 2019
Le "branding" et l'aménagement du territoire à Oman, *Arabian Humanities* 11.
DOI: 10.4000/cy.4241

Klinger, T. 2020
Oman: une politique de logement pour forger un état-nation moderne, *NAQD* 38-39/1, 141–171. DOI: 10.3917/naqd.038.0141

Klinger, T. 2021
L'Oman contemporain: Aménagement du territoire et identité nationale, Berlin.

Maneval, S. 2019
New Islamic urbanism. The architecture of public and private space in Jeddah, Saudi Arabia, London.

Mershen, B. 1998
Settlement space and architecture in South Arabian oases – ethnoarchaeological investigations in recently abandoned settlement quarters in inner Oman, *Proceedings of the Seminar for Arabian Studies* 28, 201-213.

Siegfried, N. A. 2005
La loi fondamentale omanaise: Changement ou continuité? *Égypte/Monde Arabe* 2/2, 191–212. DOI: 10.4000/ema.1742

Strother, Z. S. 2004
Architecture against the state: The virtues of impermanence in the Kibulu of Eastern Pende Chiefs in Central Africa, *Journal of the Society of Architectural Historians* 63/3), 272–295. DOI: 10.2307/4127972.

Valeri, M. 2007
Le Sultanat d'Oman: Une révolution en trompe-l'œil, Paris.

Valeri, M. 2013
Domesticating local elites. Sheikhs, walis and state-building under Sultan Qaboos, in: S. Wippel (ed.), *Regionalizing Oman: Political, economic and social dynamics*, Dordrecht, 267–278.

Viveiros de Castro, E. 2014
Cannibal metaphysics. For a post-structural anthropology, Minneapolis.